# BOETHIUS FOR BEGINNERS

## A JOURNEY THROUGH PHILOSOPHY AND FAITH

LLOYD BLAKE

*For my Family*

Nothing is miserable unless you think it so; and on the other hand, nothing brings happiness unless you are content with it.

— BOETHIUS

# CONTENTS

# INTRODUCTION

## HISTORICAL CONTEXT

To understand Boethius, it is essential to look at the historical context in which he lived. Born around 480 AD, Boethius lived during the decline of the Roman Empire. The Western Roman Empire had fallen, and Europe was in a state of flux. This period was marked by political instability, economic hardship, and cultural transformation.

The Ostrogothic Kingdom, under the rule of Theodoric the Great, was where Boethius spent most of his life. Theodoric's rule brought a semblance of order but also a delicate balance between the Roman and Gothic traditions. Boethius, a Roman senator, found himself navigating these turbulent waters. His writings reflect a world struggling to retain its classical heritage amidst barbarian rule.

Religious tensions also defined this era. The early Christian church was asserting its influence, often clashing with remaining pagan traditions. Boethius, a Christian philosopher, had to reconcile these competing worldviews. His works often sought to bridge the gap between ancient philosophy and Christian doctrine.

Amidst this backdrop, the intellectual climate was one of preservation and transition. Scholars like Boethius were tasked with saving the remnants of Greek and Roman thought. His translations and commentaries on Aristotle and Plato were crucial for future generations. These efforts were part of a broader endeavor to maintain a connection to the classical past.

Boethius' context is essential to grasp the significance of his work. It was a time of endings and beginnings, where the past's wisdom had to be preserved for a future that seemed uncertain. His life and writings are a testament to the enduring power of philosophy and its ability to offer solace in times of turmoil.

## WHO WAS BOETHIUS?

Boethius was a philosopher, statesman, and scholar whose full name was Anicius Manlius Severinus Boethius. He was born into a noble Roman family, which gave him access to the best education of his time. From an early age, he showed a keen intellect and a passion for learning. His early studies included philosophy, mathematics, and the sciences, laying the groundwork for his later works.

As a young man, Boethius quickly rose through the ranks of Roman society. He held various important positions, including consul and senator. His political career was marked by a commitment to preserving Roman traditions and promoting justice. However, his involvement in politics also led to his downfall. Accused of treason by Theodoric, he was imprisoned and eventually executed.

Despite his political career, Boethius is best known for his contributions to philosophy. His most famous work, "The Consolation of Philosophy," was written during his imprisonment. This book, a dialogue between Boethius and Lady Philosophy, explores themes of fortune, happiness, and the nature of good and evil. It remains one of the most influential philosophical works of the Middle Ages.

Boethius was also a prolific translator and commentator. He translated many of Aristotle's works into Latin, making them accessible to the Western world. His commentaries on these texts helped preserve Greek philosophy for future generations. Boethius' efforts in this area earned him the title "the first scholastic," a precursor to the later medieval scholars who would build upon his work.

Understanding who Boethius was involves recognizing his dual legacy as both a statesman and a philosopher. His life was a blend of public service and intellectual pursuit, marked by both great achievements and tragic downfall. His works continue to inspire and challenge readers, offering insights into the human condition that remain relevant today.

## THE INFLUENCE OF ANCIENT PHILOSOPHY

Boethius' work is deeply rooted in the traditions of ancient philosophy, particularly the teachings of Plato and Aristotle. From a young age, he was immersed in their ideas, which profoundly shaped his thinking. His efforts to translate and comment on their works were driven by a desire to make these philosophies accessible to his contemporaries.

Plato's influence on Boethius is evident in his use of dialogues and the exploration of metaphysical concepts. In "The Consolation of Philosophy," the dialogue between Boethius and Lady Philosophy echoes the Socratic dialogues of Plato. This method allowed Boethius to explore complex philosophical ideas in a way that was both engaging and accessible.

Aristotle's impact on Boethius is seen in his logical and analytical approach. Boethius translated several of Aristotle's works on logic, including the "Organon," which became foundational texts in medieval education. His commentaries on these works helped shape the scholastic tradition, which dominated medieval European thought.

Boethius also drew upon the Stoic philosophers, particularly in his discussions on fortune and providence. The Stoic idea that one should remain indifferent to external circumstances and focus on inner virtue is a recurring theme in his writings. This perspective provided a framework for Boethius to cope with his own misfortunes and offer solace to others.

Neoplatonism, a philosophical system developed by Plotinus, also influenced Boethius. Neoplatonism's emphasis on the One, or the Good, as the ultimate reality, resonates with Boethius' own views on God and the nature of the divine. This synthesis of Christian theology and Neoplatonic philosophy is a hallmark of Boethius' thought.

Boethius' engagement with ancient philosophy was not merely academic. He sought to apply these timeless teachings to the challenges of his own time. By doing so, he created a bridge between the ancient world and the medieval, ensuring that the wisdom of the past would continue to enlighten future generations.

## BOETHIUS' MAJOR WORKS

Boethius' intellectual legacy is built upon a diverse body of work that spans multiple disciplines. His most celebrated work, "The Consolation of Philosophy," stands out for its profound exploration of human suffering and the search for true happiness. Written during his imprisonment, this text blends prose and poetry to create a philosophical dialogue that remains influential.

In addition to "The Consolation of Philosophy," Boethius made significant contributions through his translations and commentaries. His translations of Aristotle's logical works, including "Categories" and "On Interpretation," were pivotal in bringing Greek philosophy to the Latin-speaking world. These texts became standard readings in medieval universities and shaped the development of scholasticism.

Boethius also authored original works on logic and theology. His "De Institutione Musica," a treatise on music theory, reflects his broad intellectual interests and his belief in the interconnectedness of all knowledge. This work was highly regarded during the Middle Ages and influenced the study of music for centuries.

Another significant work is "De Consolatione Theologiae," in which Boethius addresses theological questions using philosophical methods. This text exemplifies his attempt to harmonize faith and reason, a theme that runs throughout his writings. His ability to navigate both philosophical and theological domains underscores his versatility as a thinker.

Boethius' mathematical treatises, such as "De Institutione Arithmetica," also deserve mention. These works, based on earlier Greek sources, contributed to the medieval understanding of mathematics. His systematic approach and clear exposition made complex ideas more accessible to scholars of his time.

Boethius' major works reflect his comprehensive approach to knowledge and his commitment to preserving and transmitting the intellectual heritage of antiquity. His writings span philosophy, theology, music, and mathematics, demonstrating his belief in the unity of all branches of learning. Through his works, Boethius has left an indelible mark on the intellectual history of the Western world.

## THE SIGNIFICANCE OF "THE CONSOLATION OF PHILOSOPHY"

"The Consolation of Philosophy" is Boethius' magnum opus and arguably one of the most significant philosophical works of the Middle Ages. Written during his imprisonment, the text is a profound meditation on suffering, fate, and the nature of happiness. Its enduring relevance lies in its ability to speak to the universal human condition.

At its core, "The Consolation of Philosophy" addresses the question of how to find true happiness amidst life's trials. Through a dialogue between Boethius and Lady Philosophy, the text explores the transient nature of earthly goods and the pursuit of higher, more enduring values. This philosophical journey offers readers a path to inner peace and resilience.

The work's format, alternating between prose and poetry, enhances its appeal and accessibility. The poetic sections provide emotional depth and artistic expression, while the prose offers rigorous philosophical arguments. This blend of literary styles makes the text both intellectually stimulating and aesthetically pleasing.

"The Consolation of Philosophy" also stands out for its synthesis of classical philosophy and Christian theology. While rooted in the traditions of Plato, Aristotle, and the Stoics, the work incorporates elements of Christian thought. This integration reflects Boethius' own beliefs and provides a framework for later medieval scholars who sought to reconcile ancient philosophy with Christian doctrine.

The influence of "The Consolation of Philosophy" extends beyond philosophy and theology. It has impacted literature, music, and the arts, inspiring countless writers, poets, and artists throughout the centuries. Its themes of fortune, providence, and the search for meaning continue to resonate with readers today.

The significance of "The Consolation of Philosophy" lies in its timeless exploration of human nature and the search for true happiness. Its ability to bridge the gap between ancient and medieval thought while offering insights that remain relevant today ensures its place as a cornerstone of Western intellectual tradition. Boethius' masterpiece continues to inspire and challenge readers, offering wisdom and consolation in an ever-changing world.

## THEMES AND MOTIFS IN BOETHIUS' WRITINGS

Boethius' writings are rich with themes and motifs that reflect his deep engagement with philosophical and theological questions. One of the most prominent themes is the nature of happiness. In "The Consolation of Philosophy," Boethius argues that true happiness is found not in external goods but in the cultivation of virtue and wisdom. This idea echoes the teachings of ancient philosophers and offers a timeless message about the pursuit of a meaningful life.

Another recurring theme is the concept of fortune and its fickle nature. Boethius personifies Fortune as a capricious figure who bestows and withdraws her favors without warning. This motif serves to illustrate the impermanence of worldly success and the importance of finding stability within oneself. By confronting the unpredictable nature of fortune, Boethius encourages readers to seek a deeper, more enduring source of contentment.

The interplay between fate and free will is also central to Boethius' work. He grapples with the question of how human freedom can coexist with divine providence. Through his philosophical dialogues, Boethius explores the possibility that humans can exercise free will within the framework of a divinely ordered universe. This theme reflects his attempt to reconcile classical philosophy with Christian theology.

Providence, or the idea of a divine plan, is another significant motif. Boethius presents Providence as a guiding force that oversees the cosmos, ensuring that all events ultimately contribute to a greater good. This belief provides a source of comfort and reassurance, especially in the face of personal suffering. By trusting in Providence, Boethius suggests, individuals can find peace and acceptance even in difficult circumstances.

Lastly, the theme of philosophical consolation is woven throughout Boethius' writings. He views philosophy as a source of solace and strength, capable of offering comfort in times of distress. In "The Consolation of Philosophy," Lady Philosophy acts as a healer, guiding Boethius through his suffering and helping him to find clarity and perspective. This theme underscores the therapeutic power of philosophy and its potential to transform one's outlook on life.

The themes and motifs in Boethius' writings reflect his profound insights into the human condition. His exploration of happiness, fortune, fate, providence, and consolation offers timeless wisdom that continues to resonate with readers. Through his philosophical inquiries, Boethius provides a framework for understanding and navigating the complexities of life.

## RELEVANCE OF BOETHIUS TODAY

Boethius' philosophical insights continue to be relevant in today's world, offering timeless wisdom that can be applied to modern challenges. One of the reasons for his enduring relevance is his exploration of universal human experiences, such as suffering, happiness, and the search for meaning. These themes are as pertinent now as they were in Boethius' time, providing valuable perspectives for contemporary readers.

In a world where materialism and the pursuit of external success often dominate, Boethius' emphasis on inner virtue and true happiness offers a refreshing alternative. His argument that real contentment comes from within rather than from external goods resonates with modern movements that advocate for mindfulness, self-awareness, and personal growth. Boethius' teachings encourage individuals to look beyond superficial achievements and cultivate a deeper sense of fulfillment.

The concept of fortune and its unpredictability is another aspect of Boethius' thought that remains relevant. In an era marked by economic instability, political uncertainty, and rapid technological change, the idea that external circumstances are beyond our control can be both challenging and liberating. Boethius' advice to focus on inner stability and resilience provides a valuable coping mechanism for navigating life's uncertainties.

Boethius' reflections on fate and free will also speak to contemporary debates about determinism and personal agency. His nuanced approach, which allows for human freedom within a divinely ordered universe, offers a balanced perspective that can inform modern discussions about autonomy, responsibility, and the nature of existence. This theme invites readers to consider how they can exercise their own free will in meaningful ways.

The therapeutic aspect of Boethius' philosophy, particularly the idea of philosophical consolation, has significant relevance in today's context. As individuals and societies grapple with issues such as mental health, stress, and existential angst, Boethius' view of philosophy as a source of comfort and healing is especially pertinent. His writings suggest that engaging with philosophical ideas can provide clarity, solace, and a sense of purpose.

Boethius' relevance today lies in his ability to address enduring questions about human existence with insight and compassion. His exploration of happiness, fortune, fate, and consolation offers valuable lessons for modern life. By engaging with Boethius' thoughts, contemporary readers can find guidance and inspiration to navigate the complexities of the present and cultivate a more meaningful and fulfilling life.

# THE LIFE AND TIMES OF
# BOETHIUS

## EARLY LIFE AND EDUCATION

Boethius was born into a prominent Roman family around 480 AD. From an early age, he showed a remarkable aptitude for learning. His family ensured he received the best education available, which included studying under some of the most learned scholars of the time. This rigorous education laid the foundation for his future philosophical and literary achievements.

As a young boy, Boethius was immersed in the classical traditions of Greece and Rome. He studied subjects like grammar, rhetoric, and philosophy, which were considered essential for any educated Roman. This early exposure to the great thinkers of antiquity deeply influenced his intellectual development. Boethius was particularly drawn to the works of Plato and Aristotle, whose ideas would shape his own philosophical outlook.

Boethius' education wasn't limited to philosophy alone. He also studied the sciences, including mathematics and astronomy. These disciplines were closely connected to philosophy in the ancient world. This broad approach to learning reflected the classical ideal of a well-rounded education. It also prepared Boethius for the diverse range of subjects he would later write about.

His family's status afforded him the opportunity to travel and study in different parts of the Roman Empire. These travels exposed him to various cultures and intellectual traditions, further enriching his education. Boethius' ability to synthesize these diverse influences is evident in his later works, which blend elements of Greek, Roman, and Christian thought.

Despite his privileged upbringing, Boethius was not isolated from the political and social turmoil of his time. The fall of the Western Roman Empire and the rise of the Ostrogothic Kingdom created a complex and often unstable environment. This historical context played a significant role in shaping Boethius' life and work as he sought to navigate the challenges of a changing world.

POLITICAL CAREER

Boethius' political career began at a young age, leveraging his family's influence and his own impressive education. He quickly rose through the ranks of Roman society, becoming a senator while still in his twenties. His eloquence and intelligence made him a respected figure in the court of Theodoric the Great, the Ostrogothic king who ruled Italy at the time.

As a senator, Boethius worked to preserve Roman traditions and values in a time of great change. He believed in the importance of justice and sought to uphold the rule of law. This commitment to justice is reflected in his later philosophical writings, where he often grapples with questions of fairness and morality. His public service was guided by a strong sense of duty and a desire to contribute to the common good.

Boethius' political responsibilities grew over time. He was appointed as the Magister Officiorum, a high-ranking official responsible for managing the royal court's affairs. This position gave him significant influence and access to the inner workings of Theodoric's government. It also placed him at the center of the political intrigues and power struggles of the time.

Despite his successes, Boethius' political career was not without challenges. The delicate balance between the Roman aristocracy and the Ostrogothic rulers created tensions that often erupted into conflict. Boethius had to navigate these complexities carefully, striving to maintain harmony while advocating for his principles. His efforts to mediate between these factions reflected his deep commitment to preserving Roman culture and governance.

Boethius' political career ultimately ended in tragedy. Accused of treason against Theodoric, he was imprisoned and later executed. This dramatic turn of events marked a devastating end to his public life. However, it also set the stage for his most significant philosophical work, "The Consolation of Philosophy," written during his imprisonment. Boethius' political experiences and the challenges he faced profoundly influenced his later writings, adding depth and urgency to his philosophical inquiries.

## ACCUSATION AND IMPRISONMENT

Boethius' downfall began with accusations of conspiracy against Theodoric the Great. These charges were largely politically motivated, stemming from the intense rivalries and suspicions within the court. Boethius was accused of plotting to overthrow the king, a charge he vehemently denied. Despite his protests, he was arrested and imprisoned, marking the beginning of a dark chapter in his life.

The circumstances of Boethius' imprisonment were harsh. He was held in a cell with limited access to the outside world, cut off from his family and friends. This isolation was intended to break his spirit, but it also provided him with the solitude needed to reflect deeply on his situation. It was during this time that Boethius began writing "The Consolation of Philosophy," a work that would become his most enduring legacy.

In prison, Boethius grappled with feelings of betrayal and injustice. He struggled to understand why he, a loyal servant of the state, had been condemned so harshly. This sense of injustice is a central theme in "The Consolation of Philosophy," where Boethius seeks answers to the profound questions about fortune, fate, and the nature of good and evil. His philosophical dialogues with Lady Philosophy provided him with the strength and clarity to endure his suffering.

Boethius' writings from this period reflect a profound inner struggle. He was not only contending with the external injustices of his imprisonment but also with the internal battle to maintain his faith and integrity. His dialogue with Lady Philosophy serves as a metaphor for this inner journey as he moves from despair to understanding, finding solace in the timeless wisdom of philosophical thought.

The legacy of Boethius' imprisonment extends beyond his own life. "The Consolation of Philosophy" became one of the most influential texts of the Middle Ages, offering readers a way to find meaning and comfort in times of suffering. Boethius' personal ordeal and his philosophical reflections on it continue to resonate with those seeking to understand and overcome adversity. His imprisonment, though a tragic end to his political career, became the crucible for his greatest philosophical achievement.

## WRITINGS IN EXILE

During his imprisonment, Boethius turned to writing as a means of coping with his ordeal. His most famous work, "The Consolation of Philosophy," was penned during this time. This text is a dialogue between Boethius and Lady Philosophy, who personifies wisdom and offers comfort to the distressed philosopher. The work explores profound questions about human existence, suffering, and the pursuit of true happiness.

"The Consolation of Philosophy" is structured as a series of alternating prose and verse sections. The prose sections present philosophical arguments, while the poetic sections provide emotional and aesthetic reflections. This blend of literary styles enhances the work's appeal and accessibility. It allows Boethius to engage readers on both an intellectual and emotional level, making complex ideas more relatable.

In his writings, Boethius addresses the nature of fortune and the fickleness of worldly success. He argues that true happiness is not found in external goods but in the cultivation of inner virtue and wisdom. This theme is particularly poignant given his own circumstances, as he had lost everything he once valued. Through his dialogue with Lady Philosophy, Boethius finds a path to inner peace and resilience.

Boethius also grapples with the tension between fate and free will. He explores the idea that while human actions are influenced by external forces, individuals still possess the capacity for moral choice. This nuanced perspective allows for a reconciliation between human freedom and divine providence. Boethius' reflections on this theme have had a lasting impact on philosophical and theological thought.

The writings of Boethius during his exile reveal a mind deeply engaged with the most fundamental questions of human existence. His ability to find meaning and solace in philosophy during a time of personal crisis speaks to the enduring power of intellectual inquiry. Boethius' legacy as a writer is defined by his capacity to transform his own suffering into a source of wisdom and comfort for others. His works continue to inspire readers to seek understanding and strength in the face of adversity.

## PHILOSOPHICAL INFLUENCES

Boethius was profoundly influenced by the philosophical traditions of ancient Greece and Rome. His education immersed him in the works of Plato, Aristotle, and the Stoics, whose ideas shaped his thinking and writing. These classical influences are evident throughout his works, particularly in "The Consolation of Philosophy."

Plato's impact on Boethius is most apparent in his use of dialogues. In "The Consolation of Philosophy," the conversation between Boethius and Lady Philosophy mirrors the Socratic dialogues of Plato. This method allows Boethius to explore complex philosophical concepts in a dynamic and engaging way. Plato's emphasis on the realm of ideal forms and the pursuit of the good life also resonates in Boethius' writings.

Aristotle's influence is seen in Boethius' logical and analytical approach to philosophy. Boethius translated and commented on several of Aristotle's works, including the "Organon," a collection of texts on logic. His writings reflect Aristotle's emphasis on rational inquiry and the systematic exploration of philosophical questions. Boethius' ability to clarify and transmit these ideas was crucial in preserving Aristotle's legacy for medieval scholars.

The Stoic philosophers also left a significant mark on Boethius' thought. The Stoic teachings on the nature of fortune and the importance of inner virtue are central themes in "The Consolation of Philosophy." Boethius draws on Stoic ideas to argue that true happiness is found not in external circumstances but in the cultivation of inner strength and wisdom. This perspective provided him with a framework to endure his own misfortunes.

Neoplatonism, a later development of Platonic thought, also influenced Boethius. Neoplatonism's emphasis on the One, or the ultimate source of all reality, aligns with Boethius' own views on God and the nature of the divine. This philosophical system provided a way to integrate classical philosophy with Christian theology, a synthesis that is evident in Boethius' writings.

Boethius' philosophical influences reflect a deep engagement with the intellectual traditions of the past. His ability to synthesize these diverse ideas into a coherent and compelling body of work speaks to his intellectual prowess and creativity. By drawing on the wisdom of Plato, Aristotle, the Stoics, and the Neoplatonists, Boethius created a philosophical framework that continues to inspire and enlighten readers today.

## LEGACY AND HISTORICAL IMPACT

Boethius' legacy extends far beyond his own lifetime, influencing generations of thinkers and scholars. His works, particularly "The Consolation of Philosophy," became foundational texts in medieval education. They were widely read and commented upon, shaping the intellectual landscape of the Middle Ages and beyond.

One of Boethius' most significant contributions was his role in preserving and transmitting classical knowledge. His translations of Aristotle's works made these important texts accessible to the Latin-speaking world. Without Boethius' efforts, much of Greek philosophy might have been lost to the Western tradition. His commentaries provided a bridge between the ancient and medieval worlds, ensuring that the wisdom of the past continued to inform the present.

Boethius' influence is evident in the development of scholasticism, the dominant philosophical and theological movement of the medieval period. Scholastic thinkers, such as Thomas Aquinas, drew heavily on Boethius' works. His integration of classical philosophy with Christian theology provided a model for later scholars who sought to reconcile reason and faith. Boethius' writings on logic, in particular, were instrumental in shaping the scholastic method of inquiry.

In addition to his impact on philosophy and theology, Boethius also made significant contributions to other fields. His treatises on music and mathematics were highly regarded and influenced the study of these disciplines for centuries. Boethius' broad intellectual interests and his ability to connect different areas of knowledge exemplified the classical ideal of a well-rounded education.

Boethius' legacy is also reflected in his enduring appeal as a source of wisdom and comfort. "The Consolation of Philosophy" has been read and appreciated by countless individuals seeking solace in times of adversity. Its exploration of the nature of happiness, fortune, and the human condition continues to resonate with readers today. Boethius' ability to find meaning and strength in the face of suffering offers timeless lessons that are as relevant now as they were in his own time.

Boethius' historical impact is a testament to the enduring power of ideas. His works have influenced philosophy, theology, literature, music, and education, leaving a lasting mark on Western intellectual history. Boethius' legacy is a reminder of the importance of preserving and transmitting knowledge across generations. His writings continue to inspire and challenge readers, offering insights into the human experience that remain as profound and relevant today as they were over a thousand years ago.

## BOETHIUS IN MEDIEVAL THOUGHT

Boethius' influence on medieval thought was profound and far-reaching. His works became essential reading for scholars and students throughout the Middle Ages. "The Consolation of Philosophy," in particular, was widely studied and commented upon, shaping the intellectual and cultural life of the medieval period.

Medieval scholars saw Boethius as a bridge between the ancient and medieval worlds. His ability to synthesize classical philosophy with Christian theology provided a model for later thinkers. Boethius' writings were used as textbooks in the newly emerging universities, where they formed the basis for the study of philosophy and theology. His translations and commentaries on Aristotle were especially important, as they made Greek philosophy accessible to a Latin-speaking audience.

Boethius' influence extended beyond the realm of academia. His ideas permeated medieval literature, art, and music. The themes and motifs in "The Consolation of Philosophy" inspired poets, writers, and artists. The dialogue between Boethius and Lady Philosophy, with its exploration of fortune, happiness, and the nature of good and evil, resonated with the medieval imagination. Boethius' work provided a framework for understanding the human condition and the search for meaning.

In the field of theology, Boethius' writings were highly influential. His efforts to harmonize reason and faith provided a foundation for the scholastic tradition. Medieval theologians, such as Thomas Aquinas, drew on Boethius' works to develop their own ideas. Boethius' exploration of the nature of God, providence, and free will offered a philosophical basis for theological inquiry. His ability to integrate classical philosophy with Christian doctrine made his works indispensable to medieval thinkers.

Boethius' legacy in medieval thought is also evident in the way his works were preserved and transmitted. Manuscripts of "The Consolation of Philosophy" and his other writings were copied and circulated widely. These texts were treasured by medieval scholars and served as a vital link to the intellectual heritage of antiquity. Boethius' influence can be seen in the marginal notes and commentaries that medieval scribes added to these manuscripts, reflecting the ongoing engagement with his ideas.

Boethius' impact on medieval thought is a testament to the enduring relevance of his works. His ability to bridge the ancient and medieval worlds, and to synthesize diverse intellectual traditions, made him a pivotal figure in the history of Western thought. Boethius' writings continue to inspire and inform scholars, offering insights into the human condition that remain as relevant today as they were in the Middle Ages. His legacy is a reminder of the power of ideas to transcend time and shape the course of history.

# THE CONSOLATION OF PHILOSOPHY - AN OVERVIEW

## STRUCTURE AND FORMAT

"The Consolation of Philosophy" is a unique work, both in its structure and its format. Written during Boethius' imprisonment, the book is divided into five books, each containing a mix of prose and verse. This alternating format gives the work a dynamic feel, blending philosophical discourse with poetic reflections. The structure allows Boethius to delve deeply into complex ideas while also engaging the reader emotionally.

Each book within "The Consolation of Philosophy" tackles different aspects of Boethius' existential crisis. The first book sets the stage, introducing Boethius' lamentations and his encounter with Lady Philosophy. Subsequent books build on this foundation, exploring themes like fortune, happiness, and the nature of good and evil. This progression mirrors a journey from despair to enlightenment, reflecting Boethius' own search for understanding.

The use of dialogue is central to the book's structure. Boethius converses with Lady Philosophy, who guides him through his philosophical inquiries. This conversational format makes the text more accessible and engaging, as readers can follow the back-and-forth exchange of ideas. It also allows Boethius to present multiple perspectives, enriching the philosophical discussion.

The prose sections of the book are dense with philosophical arguments. Boethius draws on the works of Plato, Aristotle, and the Stoics, weaving their ideas into his own reflections. These sections are complemented by the poetic passages, which provide a more personal and emotional counterpoint. The poetry often summarizes or amplifies the themes discussed in the prose, creating a harmonious balance between intellect and emotion.

Overall, the structure and format of "The Consolation of Philosophy" are key to its enduring appeal. The blend of prose and verse, the use of dialogue, and the thoughtful progression of ideas all contribute to a work that is both intellectually rigorous and emotionally resonant. Boethius' careful construction of the text ensures that it remains a compelling read, inviting readers to engage deeply with its philosophical insights.


PHILOSOPHICAL DIALOGUES

The heart of "The Consolation of Philosophy" lies in its philosophical dialogues. These conversations between Boethius and Lady Philosophy form the core of the work, driving its exploration of profound questions about life, fate, and happiness. The dialogues are both a method of inquiry and a narrative device, making complex ideas more accessible and engaging.

Boethius uses the dialogue format to explore different perspectives on key philosophical issues. By presenting his own doubts and questions through the character of Boethius, he creates a relatable entry point for the reader. Lady Philosophy, in turn, provides reasoned responses and guidance, helping Boethius – and the reader – navigate these challenging topics. This dynamic interaction keeps the philosophical discussion lively and thought-provoking.

The dialogues are deeply rooted in the traditions of ancient Greek philosophy. Boethius draws on the works of Plato, who famously used dialogues in his writings. This method allows for a more nuanced exploration of ideas, as the back-and-forth exchange mimics real-life philosophical debates. It also helps to clarify and refine arguments as different viewpoints are examined and tested.

One of the strengths of the dialogues is their ability to humanize philosophy. By framing philosophical inquiry as a conversation, Boethius makes it more approachable. Readers can see themselves in the character of Boethius, grappling with the same doubts and seeking the same answers. Lady Philosophy's role as a compassionate and wise guide further enhances this connection, making the abstract concepts more relatable.

The philosophical dialogues in "The Consolation of Philosophy" are not just about presenting ideas; they are about engaging the reader in a process of reflection and discovery. Through these conversations, Boethius invites readers to think deeply about their own lives and beliefs. The dialogues encourage an active engagement with philosophy, showing that it is not just a theoretical pursuit but a practical guide to living a meaningful and fulfilling life.

## BOETHIUS AND LADY PHILOSOPHY

At the center of "The Consolation of Philosophy" is the relationship between Boethius and Lady Philosophy. This dynamic duo drives the narrative and philosophical inquiry, creating a compelling and personal dialogue. Boethius, as the protagonist, represents a man in crisis, seeking understanding and solace. Lady Philosophy, his guide, embodies wisdom and reason, offering clarity and comfort.

Boethius begins the work in a state of despair, imprisoned and awaiting execution. His encounter with Lady Philosophy marks the start of his journey toward enlightenment. She appears to him in a vision, her presence bringing a sense of calm and order. Her appearance is both majestic and comforting, symbolizing the power of philosophy to provide guidance in times of distress.

Throughout their dialogues, Lady Philosophy plays the role of a mentor and healer. She listens to Boethius' grievances and gently challenges his misconceptions. Her responses are thoughtful and measured, aimed at helping Boethius regain his composure and perspective. This dynamic reflects the therapeutic aspect of philosophy, where rational discourse can lead to emotional and intellectual healing.

The interaction between Boethius and Lady Philosophy also highlights the contrast between human frailty and philosophical wisdom. Boethius' initial reactions are driven by his emotional turmoil, while Lady Philosophy remains composed and rational. Through their conversations, Boethius learns to move beyond his immediate suffering and consider broader philosophical truths. This process illustrates the transformative power of philosophical inquiry.

Lady Philosophy's role is not just to provide answers but to guide Boethius toward self-discovery. She encourages him to think critically and reflect deeply on his situation. This pedagogical approach empowers Boethius to find his own path to understanding rather than passively receiving wisdom. Their relationship exemplifies the Socratic method, where questioning and dialogue lead to greater insight and self-awareness.

## THEMES OF FORTUNE AND PROVIDENCE

One of the central themes in "The Consolation of Philosophy" is the nature of fortune and providence. Boethius explores these concepts through his dialogues with Lady Philosophy, seeking to understand the role of fate and the possibility of divine order in human affairs. These themes are particularly poignant given Boethius' own fall from political power and subsequent imprisonment.

Fortune, personified as a capricious and unpredictable force, is a key figure in Boethius' reflections. Lady Philosophy describes Fortune as a wheel that turns, bringing people from the heights of success to the depths of failure without warning. This image captures the instability and impermanence of worldly goods and positions. Boethius' own experiences of dramatic change highlight the truth of this metaphor.

Providence, on the other hand, represents a higher, divine order. Lady Philosophy explains that while Fortune governs the immediate and visible changes in our lives, Providence oversees the larger, hidden plan. This distinction helps Boethius reconcile the apparent chaos of his own situation with the belief in a just and purposeful universe. Providence assures that all events, even those that seem tragic, have a place in a greater cosmic order.

The interplay between Fortune and Providence raises questions about human agency and free will. Boethius grapples with the idea that while external circumstances may be beyond our control, our internal responses are not. Lady Philosophy encourages him to focus on cultivating inner virtues, which remain constant despite the vicissitudes of fortune. This perspective offers a path to resilience and inner peace.

Boethius' exploration of these themes provides a framework for understanding and accepting life's uncertainties. By distinguishing between the whims of Fortune and the guiding hand of Providence, he finds a way to maintain faith and hope. This philosophical approach offers readers a way to navigate their own challenges, emphasizing the importance of inner strength and perspective.

The themes of Fortune and Providence in "The Consolation of Philosophy" resonate deeply with readers across ages. They address fundamental questions about the nature of fate, the existence of a higher order, and the possibility of finding meaning in adversity. Boethius' insights into these themes continue to offer wisdom and comfort to those seeking to understand and overcome the unpredictability of life.

## INTERPLAY OF POETRY AND PROSE

"The Consolation of Philosophy" is notable for its unique blend of poetry and prose. This interplay adds a rich, multi-layered texture to the work, enhancing both its aesthetic appeal and its philosophical depth. Boethius uses poetry to complement and amplify the prose, creating a harmonious balance between rational argument and emotional expression.

The prose sections of the book are where Boethius and Lady Philosophy engage in their philosophical dialogues. These parts are dense with logical reasoning and intellectual exploration. Boethius draws on classical philosophical traditions, presenting arguments and counterarguments in a clear, structured manner. The prose serves as the foundation of the work, providing the framework for Boethius' inquiry.

In contrast, the poetic sections offer a more personal and reflective perspective. These verses often summarize or echo the themes discussed in the prose, but they do so in a way that appeals to the reader's emotions and imagination. The poetry provides a lyrical counterpoint to the rational discourse, capturing the beauty and complexity of the philosophical ideas. It also allows Boethius to express his own feelings and experiences more directly.

The alternating structure of prose and poetry creates a dynamic rhythm in the text. This variation keeps the reader engaged, as the shifts in style and tone provide a refreshing change of pace. The poetry breaks up the more demanding prose sections, offering moments of reflection and contemplation. This interplay mirrors the balance between thought and emotion, reason and feeling, that Boethius seeks to achieve.

The use of poetry also enhances the accessibility of the work. While the prose delves into complex philosophical arguments, the poetry distills these ideas into more concise and evocative forms. This makes the central themes more approachable, allowing readers to connect with them on a deeper, more intuitive level. The poetry's use of imagery and metaphor also enriches the reader's understanding, providing new insights into the philosophical concepts.

The interplay of poetry and prose in "The Consolation of Philosophy" is one of the work's most distinctive features. It reflects Boethius' belief in the importance of balancing rational inquiry with emotional and aesthetic expression. This blend of styles not only enhances the work's literary quality but also deepens its philosophical impact. By engaging both the mind and the heart, Boethius creates a work that resonates on multiple levels, offering a profound and holistic exploration of life's deepest questions.

## PHILOSOPHICAL ARGUMENTS PRESENTED

"The Consolation of Philosophy" is a treasure trove of philosophical arguments. Boethius uses his dialogues with Lady Philosophy to explore a wide range of topics, from the nature of happiness to the problem of evil. These discussions are not only intellectually rigorous but also deeply personal, reflecting Boethius' own struggles and insights.

One of the central arguments in the book is the nature of true happiness. Lady Philosophy argues that true happiness is found not in external goods, such as wealth, power, or fame, but in the cultivation of inner virtues. This idea is rooted in the teachings of the ancient philosophers, particularly the Stoics, who emphasized the importance of inner resilience and moral integrity. Boethius' own fall from power underscores the fleeting nature of external success and the enduring value of inner strength.

Another key argument is the relationship between fate and free will. Boethius grapples with the question of how human freedom can coexist with divine providence. Lady Philosophy explains that while our actions are influenced by external circumstances, we still possess the ability to choose how we respond. This perspective allows for a reconciliation between the apparent determinism of fate and the autonomy of individual will. It offers a way to find meaning and agency even in difficult situations.

Boethius also addresses the problem of evil and suffering. He questions why a just and benevolent God would allow suffering to exist. Lady Philosophy responds by explaining that suffering can have a purpose within the larger framework of divine providence. It can be a means of personal growth and moral development, helping individuals to cultivate virtues and achieve a deeper understanding of themselves and the world. This view provides a way to find meaning and hope in the face of adversity.

The nature of fortune is another important theme. Lady Philosophy describes fortune as a wheel that constantly turns, bringing both good and bad times. This metaphor captures the unpredictability and impermanence of external circumstances. Boethius learns to accept the ups and downs of fortune with equanimity, focusing instead on the stability and constancy of inner virtues. This perspective encourages a shift from external to internal sources of happiness and resilience.

The philosophical arguments presented in "The Consolation of Philosophy" are both timeless and deeply relevant. They address fundamental questions about human existence, offering insights that continue to resonate with readers today. Boethius' ability to weave these arguments into a compelling narrative makes his work a powerful and enduring contribution to philosophical thought. His reflections on happiness, fate, suffering, and fortune provide a framework for understanding and navigating the complexities of life.

## IMPACT ON LATER LITERATURE

"The Consolation of Philosophy" has had a profound impact on later literature. Its themes, structure, and style have inspired countless writers, poets, and thinkers over the centuries. The work's blend of philosophical inquiry and literary artistry has made it a touchstone for those seeking to explore the human condition.

One of the most significant ways the book has influenced literature is through its themes of fortune and providence. These ideas have resonated with writers from different eras and cultures, appearing in works as diverse as Chaucer's "The Canterbury Tales" and Shakespeare's plays. The image of Fortune's wheel, in particular, has become a powerful symbol of the unpredictability of life, used by many authors to explore the highs and lows of human experience.

The structure of "The Consolation of Philosophy," with its mix of prose and verse, has also inspired literary experimentation. Writers have borrowed this format to create works that blend different genres and styles. The interplay of poetry and prose in Boethius' work demonstrates the power of combining rational argument with emotional expression, a technique that has been adopted by many subsequent authors.

The character of Lady Philosophy has also left a lasting mark on literature. Her role as a wise and compassionate guide has influenced the portrayal of similar figures in later works. Characters who embody wisdom and provide guidance to the protagonist can be seen in literature ranging from Dante's "Divine Comedy" to modern self-help books. Lady Philosophy's blend of intellectual rigor and empathetic support serves as a model for these mentor figures.

"The Consolation of Philosophy" has also been a source of inspiration for philosophical and theological writings. Its integration of classical philosophy with Christian theology provided a framework for medieval scholasticism and influenced thinkers like Thomas Aquinas and Anselm of Canterbury. The work's exploration of the relationship between reason and faith continues to inform contemporary philosophical and theological debates.

The impact of "The Consolation of Philosophy" on later literature is a testament to its enduring power and relevance. Its themes of fortune, providence, and the search for true happiness continue to resonate with readers and writers alike. Boethius' ability to blend philosophical depth with literary artistry has ensured that his work remains a vital and influential part of the Western literary canon. Through its profound insights and compelling narrative, "The Consolation of Philosophy" continues to inspire and challenge those who seek to understand the complexities of human existence.

# THE NATURE OF HAPPINESS

## DEFINING TRUE HAPPINESS

True happiness is a concept that has puzzled philosophers for centuries. Boethius, in his work "The Consolation of Philosophy," dives deep into this question. He begins by differentiating between temporary pleasures and lasting joy. True happiness, he argues, is not something that comes and goes with changing circumstances. Instead, it is a state of inner peace and contentment.

Boethius suggests that true happiness is not found in external things. Wealth, power, and fame are often seen as sources of happiness, but they are fleeting and unreliable. These external goods can be taken away, leaving a person just as empty as before. True happiness, according to Boethius, must be something that remains constant regardless of external circumstances.

For Boethius, true happiness is closely linked to the idea of the highest good. This highest good is something that is inherently valuable and cannot be lost or diminished. It is something that fulfills the deepest desires of the human heart. Boethius believes that this highest good is found in the pursuit of wisdom and virtue.

The pursuit of true happiness, then, is a journey inward. It requires a person to look beyond the superficial and seek out what is truly meaningful. This journey is not always easy, but it is ultimately rewarding. True happiness is not a fleeting pleasure but a deep and lasting fulfillment.

Boethius' definition of true happiness challenges us to reconsider our own lives. It encourages us to look beyond the immediate and the temporary and seek out what is truly valuable. In doing so, we can find a sense of peace and contentment that endures even in the face of life's challenges.

## FALSE GOODS AND THEIR DECEPTION

Boethius warns about the deception of false goods. These are things that people often mistake for sources of true happiness but which ultimately leave them unfulfilled. Wealth, for example, is one such false good. Many people believe that having a lot of money will make them happy, but Boethius points out that wealth can easily be lost and does not bring lasting satisfaction.

Another false good is power. People often strive for positions of authority, thinking that being in control will make them happy. However, Boethius argues that power is precarious and can lead to anxiety and fear. Those who are in power often live in constant worry about losing their position, which undermines any happiness they might have.

Fame is also a deceptive good. The admiration of others can feel gratifying, but it is ultimately shallow. Fame depends on the opinions of others, which can change quickly. Boethius suggests that seeking validation from others is a dangerous path to happiness, as it puts one's sense of worth in the hands of others.

Physical pleasures are another category of false goods. While these can provide temporary enjoyment, they do not lead to lasting happiness. Boethius points out that physical pleasures are fleeting and can often lead to a desire for more, creating a cycle of craving and dissatisfaction.

Boethius' critique of false goods challenges us to look deeper. It asks us to consider whether the things we are pursuing will bring us true happiness or just temporary pleasure. By recognizing the limitations of these false goods, we can redirect our efforts toward more meaningful and lasting sources of fulfillment.

## THE ROLE OF VIRTUE

For Boethius, virtue plays a central role in achieving true happiness. Virtue, he argues, is the foundation of a good and fulfilling life. It involves living in accordance with reason and striving for moral excellence. Virtue is not about achieving perfection but about consistently aiming to do what is right and good.

One key virtue that Boethius emphasizes is wisdom. Wisdom involves understanding the true nature of things and making decisions based on this understanding. It is about seeing beyond the surface and recognizing what is truly valuable.

Wisdom guides us in making choices that lead to true happiness.

Another important virtue is courage. Courage is the strength to face challenges and adversity without being overcome by fear. It involves standing firm in one's convictions and doing what is right even when it is difficult. Courage allows us to persevere in the pursuit of happiness despite the obstacles we may encounter.

Justice is also a crucial virtue in Boethius' philosophy. Justice involves treating others fairly and with respect. It is about recognizing the inherent worth of every person and acting in ways that promote the common good. Justice ensures that our pursuit of happiness does not come at the expense of others.

Lastly, temperance is a virtue that Boethius highlights. Temperance is about self-control and moderation. It involves regulating our desires and impulses so that we do not become enslaved to them. Temperance helps us to maintain balance in our lives and avoid the pitfalls of excess.

The role of virtue in achieving true happiness is a powerful message. It reminds us that happiness is not just about what we have but about how we live. By cultivating virtues like wisdom, courage, justice, and temperance, we can build a foundation for a life of true and lasting happiness.

## BOETHIUS' ARGUMENT AGAINST MATERIALISM

Boethius presents a strong argument against materialism, the idea that wealth and possessions are the keys to happiness. He observes that material goods are inherently unstable and can be lost or taken away. Relying on them for happiness is like building a house on sand; it is a fragile foundation that can crumble at any moment.

Materialism, according to Boethius, leads to a constant state of anxiety. Those who base their happiness on possessions are always worried about losing them. This fear undermines any sense of security or contentment they might have. Instead of bringing peace, materialism creates a never-ending cycle of acquisition and loss.

Furthermore, Boethius argues that material goods do not satisfy the deeper needs of the human soul. While they can provide temporary pleasure, they do not fulfill our longing for meaning and purpose. True happiness, he suggests, comes from within and cannot be bought or sold. It is found in the pursuit of wisdom and virtue, not in the accumulation of wealth.

Boethius also points out that materialism can lead to ethical and moral compromises. In the pursuit of wealth, people may engage in dishonest or harmful behavior. This not only harms others but also erodes one's own integrity and self-respect. True happiness cannot be achieved through actions that undermine our moral character.

Boethius' critique of materialism is a call to reevaluate our priorities. It challenges us to look beyond the superficial and seek out what is truly meaningful. By focusing on inner virtues rather than external possessions, we can find deeper and more lasting happiness.

## PHILOSOPHICAL PERSPECTIVES ON JOY

Joy, from a philosophical perspective, is more than just a fleeting emotion. It is a profound sense of well-being and fulfillment that arises from living a good life. Boethius explores different philosophical perspectives on joy, drawing on the insights of ancient thinkers like Plato, Aristotle, and the Stoics.

Plato's view of joy is closely tied to the pursuit of the Good. For Plato, true joy comes from aligning oneself with the highest principles of truth and justice. This involves seeking knowledge and living in harmony with the eternal forms. Joy is the natural result of a life lived in accordance with these higher ideals.

Aristotle, on the other hand, sees joy as the result of virtuous activity. He argues that happiness (or eudaimonia) is found in the practice of virtue. When we act in accordance with reason and develop our moral character, we experience deep and lasting joy. This joy is not dependent on external circumstances but is rooted in our own actions and choices.

The Stoics offer another perspective on joy. They believe that true joy comes from inner tranquility and the acceptance of what we cannot control. By cultivating an attitude of detachment and focusing on our own virtues, we can achieve a state of serenity that is impervious to external events. This inner peace is the essence of Stoic joy.

Boethius synthesizes these perspectives, suggesting that joy is found in the pursuit of wisdom and virtue. It is not about seeking pleasure or avoiding pain but about living in alignment with our true nature. Joy arises when we fulfill our potential as rational and moral beings.

These philosophical perspectives on joy provide a rich framework for understanding happiness. They remind us that true joy is not about chasing after external rewards but about cultivating inner virtues. By following the paths laid out by Plato, Aristotle, and the Stoics, we can find a deeper and more enduring sense of fulfillment.

## HAPPINESS IN ADVERSITY

Boethius' own life was marked by significant adversity, yet he found a way to maintain a sense of happiness and peace. He argues that true happiness is not dependent on external circumstances but is an inner state that can be cultivated even in the face of hardship. This perspective offers a powerful lesson in resilience and the power of the human spirit.

One of the key insights Boethius offers is the importance of perspective. Adversity can often seem overwhelming, but how we view our challenges can make a significant difference. By seeing difficulties as opportunities for growth and learning, we can transform our experiences of suffering into sources of strength and wisdom. This shift in perspective is essential for finding happiness in adversity.

Boethius also emphasizes the role of acceptance. Fighting against what we cannot change only leads to frustration and despair. By accepting our circumstances and focusing on what we can control, we can find a sense of peace. This acceptance is not about resignation but about recognizing the limits of our power and focusing our energy on positive actions.

The cultivation of inner virtues is another crucial aspect of finding happiness in adversity. Virtues like courage, patience, and resilience enable us to face challenges with grace and strength. These qualities help us to navigate difficult times and emerge stronger. Boethius' emphasis on virtue reminds us that happiness is about who we are, not what we have.

Support from others is also vital. Boethius found solace in philosophy, but he also recognized the importance of community and companionship. Sharing our burdens with others and drawing on their support can provide comfort and encouragement. This sense of connection and solidarity is a crucial part of finding happiness in difficult times.

Boethius' reflections on happiness in adversity are a testament to the power of the human spirit. They show us that even in the darkest times, we can find light and hope. By cultivating a positive perspective, accepting our circumstances, developing inner virtues, and seeking support from others, we can find a sense of peace and happiness that endures.

## RELEVANCE TO MODERN LIFE

Boethius' insights into the nature of happiness are as relevant today as they were in his own time. In a world that often emphasizes material success and external achievements, his message about the importance of inner virtues and true happiness offers a refreshing perspective. Boethius' teachings encourage us to look beyond the superficial and seek out what is truly meaningful.

One of the key lessons from Boethius is the importance of focusing on what we can control. In modern life, we are often bombarded with stresses and challenges that seem beyond our control. Boethius' emphasis on acceptance and resilience reminds us that we can find peace by focusing on our own actions and attitudes. This perspective can help us navigate the complexities of contemporary life with greater ease and confidence.

Boethius' critique of materialism is particularly pertinent in today's consumer-driven society. We are often encouraged to believe that happiness comes from acquiring more wealth and possessions. However, Boethius' argument that true happiness is found within challenges this notion. His teachings encourage us to seek fulfillment in personal growth, relationships, and the pursuit of wisdom rather than material goods.

The role of virtue in achieving happiness is another timeless lesson from Boethius. In a world where ethical and moral challenges abound, his emphasis on cultivating virtues like wisdom, courage, and justice is more important than ever. These virtues provide a foundation for a good life, helping us to make ethical decisions and contribute positively to our communities.

Boethius' reflections on happiness in adversity offer valuable insights for dealing with modern challenges. Whether we are facing personal hardships or global crises, his teachings remind us that we can find strength and resilience within ourselves. By adopting a positive perspective, accepting our circumstances, and developing our inner virtues, we can find a sense of peace and happiness that endures.

Boethius' insights into the nature of happiness are deeply relevant to modern life. They offer a powerful antidote to the superficial values of consumer culture and provide a roadmap for achieving true and lasting fulfillment. By embracing Boethius' teachings, we can find a deeper sense of purpose and contentment in our own lives.

# FORTUNE AND ITS INFLUENCE

## CONCEPT OF FORTUNE

Fortune is a powerful concept in Boethius' writings. He describes it as a force that controls the ups and downs of life. Fortune can bring success and happiness in one moment and then take it all away in the next. This unpredictability makes Fortune a central theme in understanding human experiences. Boethius personifies Fortune as a fickle and unreliable entity, constantly changing the circumstances of people's lives.

Fortune, according to Boethius, is not something we can control. It operates independently of our actions and desires. This makes it both fascinating and frustrating. People often blame or credit Fortune for their circumstances, but Boethius suggests that this is a misunderstanding. Fortune is not driven by logic or fairness; it is simply a part of life that everyone must deal with.

The idea of Fortune challenges the notion that we can plan and predict our lives. Despite our best efforts, we are always subject to the whims of Fortune. This can be unsettling, but it also forces us to develop resilience. Boethius' concept of Fortune encourages us to focus on how we respond to changes rather than trying to control them.

Boethius also uses the concept of Fortune to explain the impermanence of worldly goods. Wealth, power, and status are all subject to Fortune's influence. They can be gained and lost without warning. This perspective helps Boethius argue that true happiness cannot depend on these external factors. Instead, it must come from within.

Understanding Fortune is key to understanding Boethius' philosophy. It sets the stage for his discussions on resilience, acceptance, and the pursuit of true happiness. By acknowledging the role of Fortune in our lives, we can better navigate its challenges and uncertainties.

## FORTUNE'S WHEEL

One of the most famous images in Boethius' work is the Wheel of Fortune. This metaphor illustrates how Fortune operates in a cyclical and unpredictable manner. The wheel is always turning, bringing people from positions of power and wealth to states of poverty and despair, and vice versa. No one stays at the top or bottom forever.

The Wheel of Fortune highlights the transient nature of external success. It reminds us that what goes up must come down. This image helps Boethius convey the idea that relying on Fortune for happiness is risky and unreliable. The wheel's constant motion symbolizes the ever-changing circumstances of life.

Boethius uses the Wheel of Fortune to teach a lesson about humility and resilience. Those who find themselves at the top should not become complacent or arrogant because their position is not guaranteed. Similarly, those at the bottom should not lose hope because their fortunes can improve. The wheel's turning is a reminder that change is a constant in life.

The Wheel of Fortune also challenges the notion of meritocracy. It suggests that success and failure are not always the results of one's efforts or abilities. Instead, they can be the product of Fortune's arbitrary movements. This perspective encourages a more compassionate view of others' circumstances and a greater appreciation for one's own position.

In essence, the Wheel of Fortune serves as a powerful reminder of life's unpredictability. It teaches us to remain grounded and adaptable, knowing that our circumstances can change at any moment. Boethius' use of this metaphor underscores the importance of seeking stability and happiness within ourselves rather than in the external world.

ACCEPTANCE AND RESILIENCE

Acceptance and resilience are crucial themes in Boethius' philosophy. Faced with the unpredictability of Fortune, Boethius argues that we must learn to accept what we cannot change. This acceptance is not about resignation but about recognizing the limits of our control and focusing on our responses to life's challenges.

Boethius believes that true strength comes from within. By developing inner virtues like wisdom and courage, we can withstand the ups and downs of Fortune. This inner resilience allows us to maintain our sense of self and purpose even when external circumstances are unfavorable. It's about finding stability in a world that is constantly changing.

Resilience involves adapting to new situations and finding ways to thrive despite adversity. Boethius emphasizes the importance of flexibility and perseverance. When we accept that change is inevitable, we can better prepare ourselves to handle it. This mindset helps us to recover from setbacks and continue moving forward.

Acceptance also means letting go of anger and frustration. Boethius suggests that these emotions are natural but ultimately unproductive. By accepting our circumstances, we can focus our energy on constructive actions rather than getting stuck in negative feelings. This shift in perspective can lead to greater peace and contentment.

In practice, acceptance and resilience are about balance. They involve recognizing when to fight for change and when to adapt to what we cannot change. Boethius' philosophy teaches us that while we may not control Fortune, we can control how we respond to it. This approach empowers us to navigate life's challenges with grace and strength.

## BOETHIUS' PERSONAL REFLECTIONS

Boethius' personal reflections on Fortune are deeply intertwined with his own life experiences. As a respected philosopher and statesman, he enjoyed a position of influence and success. However, his sudden fall from grace and subsequent imprisonment profoundly shaped his views on Fortune and resilience.

In his writings, Boethius often reflects on the unpredictability of his own life. He went from being a trusted advisor to Theodoric the Great to being accused of treason and facing execution. This dramatic reversal of fortune forced him to confront the harsh realities of life and the limitations of human control.

Boethius' reflections reveal a deep sense of betrayal and disillusionment. He struggled to understand why such misfortune had befallen him despite his loyalty and service. These personal challenges prompted him to seek answers through philosophy. His dialogues with Lady Philosophy in "The Consolation of Philosophy" are a testament to his quest for understanding and inner peace.

Through his personal reflections, Boethius came to realize that true happiness could not depend on external circumstances. His own experiences of loss and suffering led him to the conclusion that inner virtues were the only reliable source of fulfillment. This realization is a central theme in his work and offers a powerful message of resilience and hope.

Boethius' personal journey underscores the universal nature of his teachings. His reflections resonate with readers who have faced their own trials and uncertainties. By sharing his struggles and insights, Boethius provides a roadmap for finding strength and meaning in the face of adversity. His personal reflections make his philosophical ideas all the more compelling and relatable.

## PHILOSOPHICAL RESPONSES TO MISFORTUNE

Boethius explores various philosophical responses to misfortune, offering insights into how we can cope with life's challenges. One approach is to focus on the impermanence of external circumstances. By recognizing that misfortune is temporary and changeable, we can maintain hope and perspective.

Another response is to cultivate inner virtues like wisdom, courage, and patience. These qualities help us navigate difficult times with grace and resilience. Boethius emphasizes that while we may not control our circumstances, we can control our responses. This inner strength enables us to endure and overcome adversity.

Boethius also highlights the importance of community and support. Sharing our burdens with others can provide comfort and encouragement. Philosophical discussions, like those Boethius has with Lady Philosophy, can help us gain new perspectives and insights. This sense of connection and solidarity is vital for coping with misfortune.

Acceptance is another key response. Boethius suggests that fighting against what we cannot change only leads to frustration. By accepting our circumstances and focusing on what we can control, we can find peace and contentment. This acceptance is not about giving up but about recognizing the limits of our power and working within them.

Lastly, Boethius advocates for finding meaning in suffering. He suggests that misfortune can be an opportunity for growth and self-discovery. By reflecting on our experiences and learning from them, we can transform suffering into a source of strength and wisdom. This perspective helps us to see misfortune not as a curse but as a part of the human journey.

## LADY PHILOSOPHY'S TEACHINGS

Lady Philosophy is a central figure in Boethius' "The Consolation of Philosophy." She serves as a guide and mentor, helping Boethius navigate his misfortunes and find inner peace. Her teachings are rooted in classical philosophy, drawing on the wisdom of Plato, Aristotle, and the Stoics.

One of Lady Philosophy's key teachings is the importance of perspective. She encourages Boethius to see his situation in a broader context. By taking a step back and looking at the bigger picture, he can gain a more balanced and less emotional view of his circumstances. This shift in perspective is crucial for finding peace and resilience.

Lady Philosophy also emphasizes the distinction between what we can control and what we cannot. She teaches Boethius to focus on his own actions and attitudes rather than external events. This focus on inner control helps him develop resilience and maintain his sense of self-worth even in the face of adversity.

Another important teaching is the value of inner virtues. Lady Philosophy encourages Boethius to cultivate qualities like wisdom, courage, and patience. These virtues provide a stable foundation for happiness and fulfillment, regardless of external circumstances. By developing these inner strengths, Boethius can find a sense of peace and purpose.

Lady Philosophy also helps Boethius understand the nature of Fortune. She explains that Fortune is inherently unpredictable and beyond human control. By accepting this reality, Boethius can let go of his frustration and focus on what truly matters. This acceptance is a key step in finding inner peace and resilience.

Through her teachings, Lady Philosophy provides Boethius with a roadmap for navigating life's challenges. Her guidance helps him transform his suffering into a source of strength and wisdom. Lady Philosophy's teachings offer timeless insights into the nature of happiness, resilience, and the human condition.

## FORTUNE IN HISTORICAL CONTEXT

Understanding Fortune in its historical context adds depth to Boethius' reflections. In ancient and medieval thought, Fortune was often personified as a capricious goddess. She was seen as a force that could grant or take away wealth, power, and happiness without warning. This view of Fortune reflects the uncertainties of life in those times.

Fortune's influence was a common theme in classical literature. Writers like Homer and Virgil depicted characters whose fates were subject to Fortune's whims. This literary tradition shaped the way people understood their own lives. Fortune was both feared and revered, a reminder of the unpredictable nature of existence.

In medieval times, the concept of Fortune was intertwined with religious beliefs. People saw Fortune as part of God's divine plan, a way of testing and shaping human character. This perspective added a moral dimension to the idea of Fortune. Misfortune was seen as a test of faith and virtue, an opportunity to demonstrate resilience and piety.

Boethius' reflections on Fortune are deeply rooted in this historical context. He draws on classical and medieval ideas to develop his own philosophy. By personifying Fortune and exploring her influence, Boethius connects his personal experiences to a broader cultural tradition. This historical perspective enriches his insights and makes them more relatable.

Understanding Fortune in its historical context helps us appreciate the depth and significance of Boethius' work. It shows how his reflections are part of a long tradition of philosophical and literary inquiry. By situating his ideas within this tradition, Boethius offers timeless insights into the nature of human experience and the search for meaning in a changing world.

# THE ROLE OF PROVIDENCE

## DEFINING PROVIDENCE

Providence is a concept that suggests a divine plan guiding the universe. Unlike Fortune, which is random and unpredictable, Providence is orderly and purposeful. It implies that there is a higher power or intelligence that oversees the world and ensures that everything happens for a reason. This idea can provide comfort, suggesting that there is meaning behind life's events, even if we don't always understand it.

Boethius sees Providence as the wisdom of God. It is the way that God governs the world, ensuring that everything fits into a grand design. This doesn't mean that bad things don't happen, but rather that all events, both good and bad, have a place in the larger scheme. Providence assures us that there is a reason for everything, even if it's beyond our comprehension.

Providence is not just about big, dramatic events. It also applies to the small details of our lives. According to this view, every moment is part of a divine plan. This can be a reassuring thought, as it suggests that our lives are not random or meaningless. Instead, they are part of a larger story that is being written by a higher power.

The idea of Providence raises important questions about human agency and responsibility. If everything is part of a divine plan, what role do our choices play? Boethius explores this tension, arguing that while Providence guides the overall direction of the world, individuals still have the freedom to make their own decisions. This blend of divine guidance and human freedom is a central theme in his philosophy.

In essence, Providence is about seeing the world as a place of order and purpose. It challenges us to trust that there is a reason for everything, even when life seems chaotic. By embracing the concept of Providence, we can find a sense of peace and meaning in the midst of life's uncertainties.


PROVIDENCE VS. FATE

Providence and fate are often used interchangeably, but they have distinct meanings in Boethius' philosophy. Fate refers to the sequence of events that unfold in the world. It's the chain of cause and effect that shapes our lives. Fate is about how things happen and the mechanics of the universe. It's impersonal and deterministic.

Providence, on the other hand, is the overarching plan that guides these events. It's the reason behind the sequence, the purpose that gives meaning to the chain of cause and effect. At the same time, fate deals with how Providence deals with the why. This distinction is crucial in understanding Boethius' view of the world.

In Boethius' framework, Providence is like an architect who designs a building, while fate is the construction process that follows the blueprint. The construction might face delays and problems, but it ultimately follows the plan laid out by the architect. Similarly, the events in our lives might seem chaotic, but they fit into a larger, divine plan.

This distinction helps Boethius reconcile the apparent randomness of life with the idea of a meaningful universe. Fate can seem cruel and arbitrary, but Providence assures us that there is a purpose behind it all. This dual perspective provides a way to understand suffering and adversity. While fate might bring challenges, Providence offers the hope that these challenges have a purpose.

Understanding the difference between Providence and fate allows us to see our lives in a new light. It helps us to trust that there is a bigger picture, even if we can't see it. By recognizing that our experiences are part of a divine plan, we can find greater acceptance and resilience in the face of life's ups and downs.

## THEOLOGICAL IMPLICATIONS

The concept of Providence has profound theological implications. It raises questions about the nature of God and the relationship between divine will and human freedom. For Boethius, Providence is a reflection of God's omniscience and benevolence. It suggests that God has a plan for the world and that this plan is ultimately for the good.

One implication is that God's knowledge is perfect and complete. If Providence guides the world, then God must know all events, past, present, and future. This idea can be comforting, as it suggests that nothing happens by chance and that there is divine wisdom behind everything. It also means that God's perspective is far beyond our own, encompassing all of time and creation.

Another theological implication is the idea of God's benevolence. If Providence is real, then everything that happens is part of a divine plan for good. This can help people trust that their suffering and struggles are not in vain. It offers hope that there is a purpose behind even the most difficult experiences and that this purpose is ultimately for their benefit.

However, the concept of Providence also raises challenging questions. If God is guiding everything, why is there evil and suffering in the world? Boethius addresses this by suggesting that what seems like evil from our limited perspective may have a purpose in the larger divine plan. This doesn't eliminate the reality of suffering but offers a way to understand it within a broader context.

The idea of Providence also impacts how we view our own actions. If everything is part of a divine plan, then our choices and actions must also have a role in that plan. This means that while we have free will, our decisions are part of the tapestry that God is weaving. This view encourages a sense of responsibility and purpose as our actions contribute to the unfolding of the divine design.

The theological implications of Providence are profound and far-reaching. They offer a way to understand the relationship between God and the world, providing comfort and hope while also challenging us to think deeply about the nature of existence and our place in it.

## HUMAN FREEDOM AND DIVINE FOREKNOWLEDGE

One of the most challenging aspects of Providence is its relationship to human freedom. If God knows everything and has a plan for the world, where does that leave human free will? This question is central to Boethius' philosophical inquiries and has significant implications for how we understand our own actions and responsibilities.

Boethius argues that human freedom and divine foreknowledge can coexist. He suggests that God's knowledge of future events does not determine those events. Instead, God knows what will happen because He is outside of time and can see all events simultaneously. This perspective allows for human freedom while maintaining the idea of a divine plan.

To illustrate this, Boethius uses the analogy of a person watching a chariot race from a high vantage point. The viewer can see the entire course and the outcome of the race, but their knowledge does not influence the decisions of the charioteers. Similarly, God's foreknowledge does not interfere with human free will; it simply observes it from a timeless perspective.

This idea of God's timeless perspective helps reconcile the tension between Providence and free will. It suggests that while God has a plan, humans still have the freedom to make their own choices within that plan. Our actions are meaningful and significant, contributing to the unfolding of the divine design.

Understanding this relationship can provide a sense of empowerment. It assures us that our choices matter and that we have a role to play in the larger story of the universe. At the same time, it offers comfort in knowing that there is a greater wisdom guiding the overall direction of our lives.

Boethius' exploration of human freedom and divine foreknowledge challenges us to think deeply about our place in the world. It encourages us to embrace our agency while trusting in the larger plan that Providence provides. This balance of freedom and trust is key to finding meaning and purpose in our lives.

## BOETHIUS' PHILOSOPHICAL DILEMMAS

Throughout his work, Boethius grapples with several philosophical dilemmas. These dilemmas reflect his attempts to understand the nature of Providence, fate, and free will. They highlight the complexities of these concepts and the challenges of reconciling them with human experience.

One of Boethius' key dilemmas is the problem of evil. If Providence guides the world for the good, why is there so much suffering and injustice? Boethius struggles with this question, especially given his own experiences of misfortune. He ultimately suggests that what seems like evil may have a purpose in the larger divine plan, even if it's beyond our understanding.

Another dilemma is the nature of human freedom. Boethius wants to affirm that humans have the ability to make meaningful choices, but he also believes in a divine plan. Reconciling these two beliefs is a significant challenge. Boethius' solution is to argue that God's foreknowledge does not constrain human actions, but this remains a complex and debated idea.

Boethius also explores the tension between reason and faith. He uses philosophical reasoning to understand Providence, but he also acknowledges the limits of human reason. This tension reflects a broader struggle to balance rational inquiry with trust in a higher power. Boethius' work embodies this balance, using reason to explore faith without claiming to fully comprehend it.

The relationship between Fortune and Providence is another area of difficulty. Boethius describes Fortune as unpredictable and often cruel, while Providence is orderly and good. Understanding how these two forces interact is a central challenge in his philosophy. Boethius suggests that Fortune operates within the framework of Providence, but this relationship remains complex and mysterious.

These philosophical dilemmas highlight the depth and difficulty of Boethius' inquiries. They show his commitment to seeking understanding, even in the face of profound challenges. Boethius' willingness to grapple with these issues makes his work both compelling and relatable as he navigates the same questions and uncertainties that many of us face.

## RECONCILIATION OF FREE WILL

Boethius' efforts to reconcile free will with Providence are among his most significant philosophical contributions. He believes that humans have genuine freedom to make choices, but he also affirms that these choices fit into a larger divine plan. This reconciliation is crucial for understanding human agency and responsibility within Boethius' framework.

One way Boethius addresses this reconciliation is by emphasizing the difference between God's perspective and ours. From our human viewpoint, the future is unknown and open to possibility. We make choices that shape our lives, and these choices feel free and unbounded. From God's timeless perspective, however, all events are known and part of a coherent plan.

Boethius argues that God's foreknowledge does not determine human actions. Instead, God's knowledge is analogous to our knowledge of past events. Just as knowing the past doesn't change what happened, God's knowledge of the future doesn't change what will happen. This analogy helps to maintain the integrity of human free will while accepting divine foreknowledge.

Another aspect of Boethius' reconciliation is his view of divine wisdom. He suggests that God's plan is so comprehensive and wise that it can incorporate human free will without contradiction. Our choices, though free, are part of the intricate design of Providence. This view respects the significance of human actions while affirming a larger order.

Boethius also touches on the moral implications of free will. He believes that true virtue requires freedom. If our actions were determined by fate, they wouldn't reflect our character or moral worth. By affirming free will, Boethius upholds the importance of personal responsibility and the possibility of genuine moral growth.

Reconciliation of free will with Providence is a complex and nuanced issue. Boethius' approach offers a thoughtful and balanced perspective, acknowledging the realities of human freedom and the guiding presence of a divine plan. This reconciliation provides a framework for understanding our actions within a meaningful and purposeful universe.

## PROVIDENCE IN CONTEMPORARY THOUGHT

The concept of Providence continues to resonate in contemporary thought. While modern perspectives might differ from Boethius' classical and medieval context, the idea of a guiding plan or purpose remains relevant. In today's world, people still seek meaning and order in the face of uncertainty and change.

One way Providence appears in contemporary thought is through the idea of destiny or life's purpose. Many people believe that their lives have a specific purpose or calling. This belief provides a sense of direction and motivation, encouraging individuals to pursue goals that align with their perceived destiny. It reflects a modern interpretation of Providence, where individuals see their lives as part of a larger plan.

In psychology, the concept of Providence can be related to the idea of a "growth mindset." This mindset involves viewing challenges and setbacks as opportunities for growth rather than as failures. It aligns with the idea of Providence by suggesting that difficulties have a purpose in personal development. This perspective helps individuals build resilience and find meaning in their experiences.

Providence also finds expression in spiritual and religious practices. Many people find comfort in the belief that a higher power is guiding their lives. This belief can provide a sense of peace and trust, especially during difficult times. It encourages individuals to see their experiences as part of a larger, meaningful story.

Contemporary philosophy and ethics also engage with the idea of Providence. Philosophers explore questions about the nature of purpose, the existence of a higher order, and the relationship between individual actions and the greater good. These discussions reflect ongoing efforts to understand how our lives fit into a broader context of meaning and value.

In modern literature and art, the theme of Providence continues to inspire. Stories and artworks often explore the tension between fate and free will, the search for meaning, and the idea of a guiding purpose. These creative expressions reflect humanity's enduring fascination with the concept of Providence and its implications for our lives.

Providence in contemporary thought shows how this ancient concept remains relevant and powerful. It provides a way to understand and navigate the complexities of modern life, offering a sense of meaning, direction, and hope. By engaging with the idea of Providence, we can find a deeper sense of purpose and resilience in our own journeys.

# THE INTERPLAY OF PHILOSOPHY
# AND RELIGION

## BOETHIUS' CHRISTIAN BACKGROUND

Boethius grew up in a Christian household, deeply influenced by the teachings of the church. His family was wealthy and well-connected, giving him access to a robust education that combined both religious and philosophical studies. Christianity wasn't just a part of his personal life; it shaped his worldview and his intellectual pursuits. This foundation would later influence his writings, especially "The Consolation of Philosophy."

In his early years, Boethius was exposed to the core tenets of Christianity. He learned about the teachings of Jesus, the importance of the Bible, and the significance of the sacraments. This religious upbringing instilled in him a sense of morality and ethics that would permeate his philosophical inquiries. His Christian faith provided a moral compass, guiding his thoughts and actions throughout his life.

Boethius' Christian background also influenced his understanding of suffering and redemption. The story of Jesus' crucifixion and resurrection offered a framework for interpreting his own experiences of hardship. In "The Consolation of Philosophy," he grapples with questions of fate and divine justice, drawing on his faith to find answers. His belief in a higher power and an afterlife provided comfort and hope during his imprisonment.

However, Boethius did not limit himself to Christian teachings. He was also deeply interested in the works of ancient Greek and Roman philosophers. This broad intellectual curiosity led him to explore how classical philosophy could complement and enhance his Christian beliefs. His goal was to create a harmonious synthesis of these two traditions, demonstrating their compatibility and mutual enrichment.

Understanding Boethius' Christian background is crucial for appreciating his work. His faith was not just a personal matter but a driving force behind his intellectual endeavors. It shaped his approach to philosophy, guiding his search for truth and meaning in a complex and often tumultuous world.

## SYNTHESIS OF GREEK PHILOSOPHY AND CHRISTIANITY

Boethius is renowned for his efforts to synthesize Greek philosophy with Christian theology. He believed that the wisdom of ancient philosophers like Plato and Aristotle could be harmonized with Christian teachings. This synthesis was not just an academic exercise but a profound attempt to bridge two rich intellectual traditions and create a more comprehensive understanding of truth.

Plato's influence on Boethius is evident in his use of dialogues and his exploration of metaphysical concepts. Plato's emphasis on the realm of forms and the pursuit of the Good resonated with Boethius' Christian beliefs about the nature of God and the soul. Boethius saw Plato's philosophy as a way to understand and articulate the divine order that Christianity teaches.

Aristotle's logical and ethical writings also played a significant role in Boethius' thought. Boethius translated and commented on many of Aristotle's works, making them accessible to the Latin-speaking world. Aristotle's focus on reason, ethics, and the nature of reality provided a robust framework for Boethius to explore theological questions. By integrating Aristotle's logic with Christian doctrine, Boethius aimed to demonstrate the rational basis of faith.

The Stoics, with their teachings on virtue and the nature of the cosmos, also influenced Boethius. The Stoic idea of living in accordance with nature and reason complemented Christian teachings on virtue and moral integrity. Boethius used Stoic principles to discuss the nature of happiness and the role of Providence, showing how these ideas could enrich Christian understanding.

Boethius' synthesis of Greek philosophy and Christianity was groundbreaking. It laid the foundation for medieval scholasticism, which sought to reconcile faith and reason. His work showed that philosophy and theology were not opposing forces but could work together to provide a deeper understanding of the world and our place in it. This synthesis remains a cornerstone of Western intellectual tradition.

By blending these traditions, Boethius created a powerful intellectual framework. His synthesis of Greek philosophy and Christianity allowed him to address complex theological questions with clarity and depth. It demonstrated that faith and reason could coexist and complement each other, offering a richer and more nuanced understanding of truth.

## PHILOSOPHICAL ARGUMENTS FOR GOD

Boethius presented several philosophical arguments for the existence of God, drawing on both Christian theology and classical philosophy. These arguments were aimed at demonstrating that belief in God was not only a matter of faith but also supported by reason and logic. His work sought to show that the existence of God could be understood through rational inquiry.

One of Boethius' key arguments is based on the concept of the highest good. He argues that there must be a supreme being who embodies the highest good, as all things strive towards this ultimate goal. This idea is rooted in Plato's philosophy, which posits that the Good is the source of all existence. Boethius uses this framework to argue that God, as the highest good, must exist to give purpose and direction to all things.

Another argument Boethius presents is the notion of a first cause. This idea, derived from Aristotle, suggests that everything in the world has a cause, and there must be an initial, uncaused cause that set everything into motion. Boethius identifies this first cause as God, the prime mover who initiates and sustains the existence of the universe. This argument provides a logical basis for the existence of a divine creator.

Boethius also explores the idea of divine intelligence. He argues that the order and complexity of the universe imply a guiding intelligence behind it. This intelligence, he suggests, is God, who designed and governs the cosmos with wisdom and purpose. This argument aligns with the teleological perspective, which sees evidence of design in the natural world as proof of a designer.

The concept of contingency is another philosophical argument Boethius uses to support the existence of God. He posits that everything in the world is contingent, meaning it depends on something else for its existence. Since there cannot be an infinite regress of contingent beings, there must be a necessary being that exists independently and sustains everything else. Boethius identifies this necessary being as God.

Boethius' philosophical arguments for God are significant because they bridge faith and reason. They provide a rational foundation for belief in God, showing that theological concepts can be explored and supported through logical analysis. His work offers a compelling case for the compatibility of philosophy and religion, demonstrating that both can contribute to a deeper understanding of the divine.


CRITIQUE OF PAGAN BELIEFS

In his efforts to harmonize Christianity with Greek philosophy, Boethius also critiqued certain pagan beliefs. His goal was to distinguish the truths found in classical philosophy from the superstitions and errors of pagan religion. This critique was part of his broader project to show that reason and faith could work together to reveal deeper truths.

Boethius challenged the polytheistic beliefs of ancient paganism. He argued that the existence of many gods was logically inconsistent with the idea of a single, ultimate source of all good. For Boethius, the concept of one God, as found in Christianity, made more sense both philosophically and theologically. He believed that the unity of God provided a clearer and more coherent understanding of the divine.

Another aspect of Boethius' critique was his rejection of pagan rituals and practices. He saw these as distractions from the pursuit of true wisdom and virtue. Pagan rituals often involved sacrifices and ceremonies aimed at appeasing various gods, but Boethius argued that true worship should focus on the contemplation of the divine and the cultivation of moral character. He believed that these practices did not lead to genuine spiritual growth.

Boethius also critiqued the pagan view of the afterlife. Many pagan religions had elaborate myths about the afterlife, involving multiple realms and deities. Boethius, drawing on Christian teachings, argued for a more straightforward and morally coherent view of the afterlife. He believed in a final judgment and the existence of heaven and hell, where souls would be rewarded or punished based on their earthly lives.

The role of fate in pagan beliefs was another target of Boethius' critique. Paganism often emphasized the power of fate and destiny, which could make life seem arbitrary and beyond human control. Boethius, however, advocated for the Christian idea of Providence, which suggested a purposeful and benevolent divine plan. This perspective offered a more hopeful and meaningful view of human existence.

Boethius' critique of pagan beliefs was not merely a rejection but an effort to refine and elevate philosophical and theological understanding. By challenging the inconsistencies and superstitions of paganism, he aimed to demonstrate the superiority of a worldview that integrated reason with the Christian faith. His critique helped to pave the way for a more rational and ethical approach to spirituality.

## FAITH AND REASON

Boethius believed that faith and reason were not opposing forces but complementary paths to truth. He argued that true understanding required both the insights of philosophy and the revelations of religion. This integration of faith and reason was central to his work and has had a lasting impact on Western thought.

Faith, for Boethius, provided the foundational truths of Christianity. These truths, such as the existence of God and the promise of salvation, were revealed through scripture and the teachings of the church. Boethius believed that faith was essential for understanding the divine and living a moral life. It provided the ultimate answers to questions about existence and purpose.

Reason, on the other hand, was the tool for exploring and understanding these truths. Boethius saw philosophy as a way to deepen and clarify religious beliefs. By using reason, individuals could better understand the nature of God, the principles of morality, and the workings of the universe. Philosophy offered a way to articulate and defend the teachings of faith.

Boethius used reason to address doubts and challenges to faith. He believed that philosophical inquiry could strengthen belief by providing logical support for religious doctrines. This approach helped to counteract skepticism and reinforce the credibility of faith. By showing that faith was reasonable, Boethius aimed to make it more accessible and compelling.

The relationship between faith and reason also involved a recognition of their respective limits. Boethius acknowledged that reason alone could not fully comprehend the mysteries of the divine. Some truths were beyond human understanding and required faith. At the same time, he believed that faith should not reject reason but embrace it as a valuable ally in the search for truth.

Boethius' integration of faith and reason set the stage for medieval scholasticism and influenced thinkers like Thomas Aquinas. His work demonstrated that religious belief could be intellectually rigorous and philosophically robust. By harmonizing faith with reason, Boethius created a powerful framework for understanding the world and our place in it.

## BOETHIUS' INFLUENCE ON MEDIEVAL THEOLOGY

Boethius' work had a profound impact on medieval theology. His efforts to integrate Greek philosophy with Christian doctrine laid the groundwork for the scholastic tradition, which sought to harmonize faith and reason. Medieval theologians built on Boethius' ideas, using his writings as a foundation for their own explorations of theology and philosophy.

One of Boethius' key contributions was his translation and commentary on Aristotle's works. These translations made Aristotle's philosophy accessible to the Latin-speaking world and provided a basis for theological inquiry. Medieval scholars, including Thomas Aquinas, used Boethius' translations to develop their own philosophical and theological systems. Aristotle's emphasis on logic and ethics influenced the way these scholars approached religious questions.

Boethius' "The Consolation of Philosophy" also had a significant impact. This work, written during his imprisonment, explored themes of fortune, suffering, and divine Providence. It became a central text in medieval education, offering insights into how to reconcile human suffering with a benevolent divine plan. Medieval theologians drew on Boethius' reflections to address the problem of evil and the nature of God's governance.

Boethius' emphasis on the compatibility of faith and reason was another important influence. His work demonstrated that philosophical inquiry could support and enhance religious belief. This idea became a cornerstone of scholasticism, which sought to use reason to understand and explain the teachings of the church. Boethius' integration of philosophy and theology provided a model for how these disciplines could work together.

Theological concepts such as the nature of God, the immortality of the soul, and the relationship between free will and divine foreknowledge were central to Boethius' work and influenced medieval thought. His philosophical arguments for the existence of God and his exploration of divine Providence provided a framework for theological discussion. Medieval scholars built on these ideas, developing more nuanced and sophisticated understandings of these concepts.

Boethius' influence on medieval theology extended beyond his writings. His life and work exemplified the pursuit of wisdom and virtue in the face of adversity. This legacy inspired medieval scholars to seek truth and understanding, even in difficult circumstances. Boethius' integration of faith and reason, his philosophical rigor, and his moral integrity made him a model for medieval theologians and philosophers.

## RELIGION'S ROLE IN "THE CONSOLATION OF PHILOSOPHY"

Religion plays a crucial role in "The Consolation of Philosophy," Boethius' most famous work. Written during his imprisonment, the book is a dialogue between Boethius and Lady Philosophy. While it primarily focuses on philosophical questions, religious themes are woven throughout, reflecting Boethius' Christian beliefs and his attempts to find meaning in his suffering.

One of the central religious themes in the book is the concept of divine Providence. Boethius grapples with the idea that a benevolent God oversees the world and ensures that everything happens for a reason. This belief provides a sense of comfort and hope, suggesting that his suffering has a purpose within a larger divine plan. Lady Philosophy helps Boethius understand that Providence is guiding his life, even when it seems chaotic.

Another important religious theme is the nature of true happiness. Boethius argues that true happiness is found in the pursuit of virtue and wisdom, which aligns with Christian teachings about the ultimate goal of human life. He suggests that material goods and worldly success are fleeting and unreliable, whereas inner virtues provide lasting fulfillment. This perspective is rooted in both philosophical reasoning and religious faith.

The problem of evil is also addressed in the book. Boethius struggles with the question of why a just and loving God allows suffering and injustice to exist. Lady Philosophy helps him see that what appears as evil may have a purpose in the divine plan, contributing to the overall good. This idea reflects the Christian belief in the redemptive power of suffering and the ultimate justice of God.

Prayer and contemplation are presented as important practices for finding peace and understanding. Boethius emphasizes the need to turn inward and seek divine guidance through prayer. This religious practice is seen as a way to connect with the divine and gain the wisdom needed to navigate life's challenges. It reflects Boethius' belief in the importance of maintaining a relationship with God.

While "The Consolation of Philosophy" is a philosophical work, its religious elements are integral to its message. Boethius uses philosophical reasoning to explore and support his Christian beliefs, demonstrating the compatibility of faith and reason. The book offers a powerful example of how religion can provide meaning and comfort in the face of adversity, guiding individuals toward a deeper understanding of themselves and the world.

# THE LEGACY OF BOETHIUS IN MEDIEVAL THOUGHT

❧

## BOETHIUS AS A TRANSITIONAL FIGURE

Boethius lived during a time of great change. The Roman Empire was falling, and Europe was entering what we now call the Middle Ages. Boethius served as a bridge between these two eras. He preserved and passed on the knowledge of the ancient world to the medieval scholars who came after him. His work helped keep the wisdom of Greece and Rome alive.

Boethius' role as a transitional figure is evident in his translations of Greek philosophy. He translated many of Aristotle's works into Latin, making them accessible to a wider audience. Without Boethius, much of Aristotle's philosophy might have been lost to the Western world. His translations were used in schools and universities for centuries.

Beyond translations, Boethius wrote original works that combined classical philosophy with Christian theology. This blending of ideas was crucial for the development of medieval thought. Boethius showed that the teachings of Plato and Aristotle could be harmonized with the doctrines of Christianity. This synthesis helped lay the groundwork for later philosophical and theological developments.

Boethius' influence extended beyond philosophy. His writings on music and mathematics were also important. He preserved and explained ancient theories, making them available to medieval scholars. His work in these fields demonstrated the interconnectedness of different areas of knowledge, a concept that was central to medieval education.

In many ways, Boethius was a pioneer. He bridged the gap between the ancient and medieval worlds, ensuring that the wisdom of the past was not lost. His efforts helped shape the intellectual landscape of the Middle Ages and beyond. Boethius' legacy as a transitional figure is a testament to his enduring impact on Western thought.

## INFLUENCE ON SCHOLASTICISM

Scholasticism was a method of learning that dominated medieval Europe. It emphasized the use of reason to understand and explain religious faith. Boethius' work was foundational for the development of this intellectual tradition. His writings provided the tools and concepts that scholastic thinkers used to explore and defend their beliefs.

Boethius' translations of Aristotle were particularly important for scholasticism. Aristotle's emphasis on logic and rational inquiry resonated with the scholastic method. Boethius' translations and commentaries helped medieval scholars understand and apply Aristotle's ideas. This integration of logic and theology was a hallmark of scholastic thought.

In addition to Aristotle, Boethius' own works were central to scholastic education. "The Consolation of Philosophy" was widely read and studied. Its exploration of themes like fortune, happiness, and divine Providence provided rich material for scholastic debate. Boethius' ability to blend philosophical reasoning with Christian doctrine served as a model for later scholars.

Boethius' influence can be seen in the work of major scholastic thinkers like Thomas Aquinas and Peter Abelard. These scholars built on Boethius' ideas, developing more sophisticated arguments and theories. Boethius' emphasis on the compatibility of faith and reason was a key theme in their writings. His work helped establish the intellectual framework for scholasticism.

The impact of Boethius on scholasticism is a testament to his lasting legacy. His translations, commentaries, and original writings provided the foundation for medieval intellectual life. Boethius' influence on scholasticism ensured that his ideas continued to shape Western thought for centuries to come.

## COMMENTARIES AND TRANSLATIONS

Boethius was not just a philosopher; he was also a translator and commentator. His translations of Greek works into Latin were crucial for preserving ancient knowledge. Boethius translated several of Aristotle's key texts, including "Categories" and "On Interpretation." These translations made Aristotle's ideas accessible to the Latin-speaking world and were used in medieval universities for centuries.

In addition to his translations, Boethius wrote commentaries on these works. His commentaries helped explain and interpret Aristotle's ideas, making them easier to understand. Boethius' insights and explanations were highly valued by medieval scholars. His commentaries provided a bridge between the ancient texts and their medieval readers.

Boethius also wrote original treatises that built on the ideas of Greek philosophers. His work "The Consolation of Philosophy" is a prime example. In this text, Boethius blends his own ideas with those of Plato, Aristotle, and the Stoics. The result is a rich and complex exploration of philosophy and theology. This work was highly influential and widely read throughout the Middle Ages.

Boethius' efforts as a translator and commentator had a lasting impact on medieval thought. His work ensured that the wisdom of the ancient world was preserved and passed on to future generations. Boethius' translations and commentaries were essential tools for medieval scholars, helping them to engage with and build on the ideas of the past.

The legacy of Boethius' translations and commentaries is still felt today. His work helped shape the intellectual landscape of the Middle Ages and laid the groundwork for the Renaissance. Boethius' contributions as a translator and commentator are a testament to his enduring impact on Western thought.

## BOETHIUS IN MONASTIC EDUCATION

Monasteries were centers of learning in medieval Europe, and Boethius' works were central to their curriculum. Monastic education emphasized the study of classical texts, and Boethius' translations and writings were among the most important. Monks studied his works to gain a deeper understanding of philosophy, theology, and the liberal arts.

"The Consolation of Philosophy" was a key text in monastic education. Its exploration of themes like fortune, happiness, and virtue resonated with the monastic emphasis on spiritual and moral development. Monks read and discussed Boethius' work as part of their intellectual and spiritual training. The text provided a framework for understanding the relationship between human suffering and divine Providence.

Boethius' translations of Aristotle were also important in monastic education. Monks studied these texts to learn about logic and natural philosophy. Aristotle's emphasis on reason and observation was seen as complementary to the monastic pursuit of knowledge and wisdom. Boethius' translations helped monks engage with these ideas and incorporate them into their own studies.

In addition to his philosophical works, Boethius' writings on music and mathematics were also studied in monasteries. His treatises on these subjects were part of the quadrivium, the higher division of the medieval curriculum. Monks used Boethius' works to learn about the mathematical and musical principles that underpinned the natural world. His writings helped to cultivate a holistic approach to education that integrated different areas of knowledge.

Boethius' influence on monastic education extended beyond his own time. His works continued to be studied and valued throughout the Middle Ages and into the Renaissance. The emphasis on classical learning in monastic education helped to preserve and transmit the wisdom of the ancient world. Boethius' contributions to this tradition are a testament to his enduring legacy.

## MEDIEVAL PHILOSOPHICAL DEBATES

Boethius' ideas played a central role in medieval philosophical debates. His writings provided a foundation for discussions on a wide range of topics, from metaphysics to ethics. Medieval scholars engaged with Boethius' works to explore and develop their own ideas. His influence can be seen in the major philosophical debates of the Middle Ages.

One of the key debates was the nature of universals. Boethius' translations and commentaries on Aristotle introduced medieval scholars to the question of whether universals exist independently of particular things. This debate, known as the problem of universals, was a central issue in medieval philosophy. Scholars like Peter Abelard and Thomas Aquinas engaged with Boethius' ideas to develop their own positions on this question.

Another important debate was the relationship between faith and reason. Boethius' emphasis on the compatibility of these two approaches to knowledge provided a framework for medieval thinkers. Scholars like Anselm of Canterbury and Thomas Aquinas used Boethius' ideas to argue that reason could be used to understand and explain religious faith. This debate helped to shape the intellectual landscape of medieval Europe.

Boethius' exploration of the nature of happiness and the role of virtue was also a key topic of debate. His writings on these subjects provided a foundation for discussions on ethics and moral philosophy. Medieval scholars engaged with Boethius' ideas to explore questions about the nature of the good life and the importance of inner virtues. His influence can be seen in the ethical theories of thinkers like Albert the Great and Bonaventure.

The problem of evil was another major debate influenced by Boethius. His reflections on why a just and loving God allows suffering and injustice provided a starting point for medieval discussions. Scholars like Augustine and Aquinas built on Boethius' ideas to develop their own theodicies. This debate remains a central issue in philosophy and theology to this day.

Boethius' contributions to medieval philosophical debates highlight the enduring relevance of his work. His ideas provided a foundation for discussions on a wide range of topics, helping to shape the intellectual landscape of the Middle Ages. Boethius' influence on these debates is a testament to his lasting impact on Western thought.

CULTURAL AND INTELLECTUAL LEGACY

Boethius' influence extends beyond philosophy and theology. His work has had a profound impact on Western culture and intellectual history. Boethius' ideas have been reflected in literature, music, and the arts, demonstrating the wide-ranging significance of his contributions.

In literature, "The Consolation of Philosophy" has been a source of inspiration for writers throughout the centuries.

Dante, Chaucer, and Shakespeare all drew on Boethius' themes and ideas in their own works. The exploration of fortune, suffering, and divine Providence in "The Consolation of Philosophy" resonated with these writers, who incorporated Boethian themes into their own stories and characters.

Boethius' influence on music is also notable. His treatise "De Institutione Musica" was one of the most important works on music theory in the Middle Ages. It provided a framework for understanding the mathematical principles of music and its relationship to the cosmos. Boethius' ideas on music were studied and taught in medieval universities, shaping the development of Western musical thought.

The visual arts have also been influenced by Boethius' work. Medieval manuscripts of "The Consolation of Philosophy" were often richly illustrated, reflecting the text's significance. Artists used these illustrations to convey Boethius' themes and ideas visually. The interplay of text and image in these manuscripts demonstrates the cultural impact of Boethius' work.

Boethius' ideas have also influenced intellectual history more broadly. His emphasis on the compatibility of faith and reason laid the groundwork for the development of Western thought. Boethius' synthesis of classical philosophy and Christian theology helped to shape the intellectual landscape of medieval Europe. His work provided a foundation for the scholastic tradition and influenced the development of modern philosophy.

The cultural and intellectual legacy of Boethius is a testament to the enduring significance of his work. His ideas have shaped literature, music, the arts, and intellectual history, demonstrating the wide-ranging impact of his contributions. Boethius' influence continues to be felt today, reflecting the timeless relevance of his thought.

## BOETHIUS AND THE RENAISSANCE

Boethius' influence extended into the Renaissance, a period of renewed interest in classical learning. Renaissance scholars looked to Boethius as a key figure who bridged the gap between the ancient and medieval worlds. His translations, commentaries, and original works were studied and valued by Renaissance thinkers who sought to revive and build on the wisdom of the past.

One of the ways Boethius influenced the Renaissance was through his translations of Aristotle. These texts were crucial for the revival of Aristotelian philosophy during the Renaissance. Scholars like Marsilio Ficino and Giovanni Pico della Mirandola studied Boethius' translations and used them to develop their own philosophical ideas. Boethius' work helped to make Aristotle's philosophy accessible to a new generation of thinkers.

"The Consolation of Philosophy" continued to be an important text during the Renaissance. Its exploration of themes like fortune, happiness, and virtue resonated with Renaissance humanists who were interested in questions about the nature of the good life. The text was widely read and commented on, and its influence can be seen in the writings of thinkers like Erasmus and Thomas More.

Boethius' integration of classical philosophy and Christian theology also had a lasting impact on Renaissance thought. Renaissance scholars sought to harmonize the wisdom of the ancient world with their own religious beliefs. Boethius' work provided a model for how this synthesis could be achieved. His emphasis on the compatibility of faith and reason was a key theme in Renaissance philosophy.

Boethius' influence on the arts continued during the Renaissance. His ideas on music, as outlined in "De Institutione Musica," shaped the development of Renaissance music theory. Composers and musicians studied Boethius' work to understand the mathematical principles underlying musical harmony. His ideas helped to shape the development of Western music during this period.

The legacy of Boethius in the Renaissance is a testament to the enduring significance of his work. His translations, writings, and ideas continued to shape Western thought and culture long after his death. Boethius' influence on the Renaissance reflects the timeless relevance of his contributions and his lasting impact on the intellectual history of the Western world.

# BOETHIUS AND THE ARTS

## BOETHIUS' INFLUENCE ON LITERATURE

Boethius' work has left a lasting mark on literature. His book "The Consolation of Philosophy" has inspired countless writers over the centuries. This text, which blends prose and poetry, tackles profound themes like fate, happiness, and the nature of good and evil. Writers have drawn from Boethius' ideas to explore similar themes in their own works.

One of the most famous writers influenced by Boethius is Geoffrey Chaucer. In "The Canterbury Tales," Chaucer references Boethius and his ideas. Chaucer's characters often grapple with the same questions Boethius explored, such as the role of fortune in human life. Boethius' themes of wisdom and virtue echo throughout Chaucer's tales, showing the deep impact of his philosophy.

William Shakespeare also shows traces of Boethius' influence. In plays like "King Lear" and "Hamlet," the characters face the whims of fortune and struggle to find meaning in their suffering. Shakespeare's exploration of these themes is reminiscent of Boethius' own philosophical inquiries. The depth and complexity of Shakespeare's characters owe much to the groundwork laid by Boethius.

Dante Alighieri, the author of "The Divine Comedy," was another writer inspired by Boethius. Dante's epic poem reflects Boethius' ideas about justice, virtue, and divine order. In "The Divine Comedy," Dante travels through Hell, Purgatory, and Heaven, exploring the consequences of human actions and the possibility of redemption. Boethius' influence can be seen in Dante's treatment of these themes.

Modern literature continues to feel Boethius' influence. Authors explore the same timeless questions about the human condition, drawing on Boethius' insights. His work remains relevant because it addresses universal themes that resonate with readers across ages. Boethius' influence on literature is a testament to the enduring power of his ideas.

PHILOSOPHICAL POETRY

Boethius was a master of philosophical poetry, blending deep ideas with lyrical expression. His use of poetry in "The Consolation of Philosophy" adds an emotional and aesthetic dimension to his philosophical arguments. The verses provide a counterpoint to the prose, offering a more personal and reflective perspective on the themes he explores.

The poetry in "The Consolation of Philosophy" often serves to summarize and highlight key philosophical points. For example, Boethius uses verses to meditate on the nature of fortune, the fleeting nature of worldly goods, and the search for true happiness. These poetic interludes allow readers to reflect more deeply on the ideas presented in the prose sections.

Boethius' use of poetry also makes his work more accessible. The lyrical quality of his verses captures the reader's imagination and emotions, making complex philosophical concepts easier to understand. The beauty of the language draws readers in, encouraging them to engage with the deeper meanings behind the words.

The influence of Boethius' philosophical poetry can be seen in the works of later poets. For instance, Dante and Petrarch both incorporate philosophical themes into their poetry, following Boethius' example. These poets use verse to explore questions about love, fate, and the divine, creating a rich tradition of philosophical poetry that traces back to Boethius.

Boethius' legacy as a philosophical poet continues to inspire modern writers. His ability to combine intellectual rigor with poetic beauty demonstrates the power of language to convey deep truths. Boethius' philosophical poetry remains a model for those who seek to express complex ideas in a way that touches both the mind and the heart.

## IMPACT ON MEDIEVAL MUSIC THEORY

Boethius made significant contributions to medieval music theory, particularly through his treatise "De Institutione Musica." This work became one of the most important texts on music in the Middle Ages. Boethius' ideas about the mathematical foundations of music influenced the way people understood and studied this art form.

In "De Institutione Musica," Boethius divides music into three categories: musica mundana (the music of the spheres), musica humana (the harmony of the human body and soul), and musica instrumentalis (instrumental music). This classification system helped medieval scholars conceptualize music as a reflection of the divine order. Boethius' emphasis on the cosmic and human aspects of music underscored its significance beyond mere entertainment.

Boethius also introduced the concept of the "quadrivium," which included music alongside arithmetic, geometry, and astronomy as essential fields of study. By placing music within this framework, Boethius elevated its status as a serious intellectual pursuit. This approach influenced the curriculum of medieval universities, where music was studied as a liberal art.

His writings on the mathematical ratios that underpin musical harmony were particularly influential. Boethius drew on the work of ancient Greek philosophers like Pythagoras, who discovered the numerical relationships between musical intervals. Boethius' explanations of these principles provided a theoretical foundation for understanding musical harmony and structure.

The impact of Boethius' music theory extended to practical applications as well. Medieval composers and musicians used his ideas to guide their work, developing compositions that adhered to the principles of harmony and proportion outlined in "De Institutione Musica." Boethius' influence can be seen in the development of Gregorian chant and other forms of medieval music.

Boethius' contributions to music theory demonstrate his interdisciplinary approach to knowledge. His work bridged the gap between mathematics and the arts, showing how music could be understood through rational inquiry. Boethius' legacy in this field highlights the enduring relevance of his ideas in shaping the intellectual and cultural landscape of the Middle Ages.

## VISUAL ARTS AND MANUSCRIPTS

Boethius's influence extends to the visual arts, particularly in the realm of illuminated manuscripts. "The Consolation of Philosophy" was a popular text in the Middle Ages, and many beautifully illustrated copies were produced. These manuscripts are a testament to the importance of Boethius' work and the impact it had on medieval culture.

Illuminated manuscripts of "The Consolation of Philosophy" often feature intricate illustrations that complement the text. These images depict scenes from Boethius' life and the allegorical figures he describes, such as Lady Philosophy and Fortune. The artwork serves to enhance the reader's understanding of the text, providing a visual representation of its themes and ideas.

The illustrations in these manuscripts reflect the medieval belief in the interconnectedness of all forms of knowledge. Just as Boethius blended philosophy and poetry, the artists who created these manuscripts combined text and images to create a unified work of art. This holistic approach to knowledge is a hallmark of medieval culture.

In addition to illuminated manuscripts, Boethius' influence can be seen in other forms of visual art. Paintings, sculptures, and stained glass windows depicting scenes from "The Consolation of Philosophy" were created throughout the Middle Ages and Renaissance. These artworks reflect the enduring appeal of Boethius' ideas and their relevance to the broader cultural and intellectual milieu.

The visual representations of Boethius' work highlight the power of art to convey complex ideas. Through images, artists were able to bring Boethius' philosophical concepts to life, making them more accessible and engaging for a wider audience. This visual dimension of Boethius' legacy underscores the enduring impact of his work on the arts.

Boethius' influence on the visual arts is a testament to the enduring power of his ideas. His work inspired artists to create beautiful and meaningful representations of his philosophical themes. The illuminated manuscripts and other artworks that feature Boethius' ideas continue to captivate and inspire, demonstrating the lasting impact of his contributions to the cultural heritage of the Western world.

## DRAMA AND PERFORMANCE

Boethius' influence extends into the world of drama and performance. His themes and ideas have been adapted into various theatrical works over the centuries. Playwrights and performers have drawn inspiration from Boethius' exploration of fate, fortune, and the search for meaning, creating dramas that resonate with audiences.

Medieval morality plays often reflected Boethian themes. These plays, which were performed in public spaces, aimed to teach moral lessons through allegorical characters and narratives. The themes of fortune's unpredictability and the importance of inner virtue, central to Boethius' work, were commonly explored in these performances. Through drama, Boethius' ideas reached a broad audience, reinforcing the cultural and moral values of the time.

During the Renaissance, playwrights like William Shakespeare incorporated Boethian themes into their works. In tragedies like "King Lear" and "Macbeth," characters grapple with the capriciousness of fortune and the consequences of their actions. These plays echo Boethius' reflections on the human condition, fate, and the pursuit of wisdom. Shakespeare's use of Boethian themes highlights the enduring relevance of these ideas in dramatic literature.

In more modern times, Boethius' influence can be seen in various adaptations of "The Consolation of Philosophy" for the stage. These adaptations bring Boethius' philosophical dialogues to life, allowing audiences to engage with his ideas in a dynamic and interactive way. The themes of suffering, redemption, and the search for truth resonate deeply in a theatrical context, demonstrating the timeless appeal of Boethius' work.

Boethius' impact on drama and performance also extends to educational settings. School plays and university productions often draw on Boethian themes, using drama as a tool for exploring philosophical and ethical questions. These performances provide a way for students to engage with Boethius' ideas in a creative and immersive manner, enhancing their understanding of his work.

The legacy of Boethius in drama and performance underscores the versatility and enduring relevance of his ideas. Through theatrical adaptations and performances, Boethius' philosophical themes continue to captivate and inspire audiences. His influence on drama highlights the power of performance to bring complex ideas to life and make them accessible to a wide audience.

## BOETHIUS IN CONTEMPORARY ARTS

Boethius' influence extends into contemporary arts, where his themes and ideas continue to inspire artists across various mediums. Modern writers, filmmakers, musicians, and visual artists draw on Boethius' exploration of fate, fortune, and the search for meaning, creating works that resonate with today's audiences.

Contemporary authors often reference Boethius' themes in their works. Novels that explore the unpredictability of life, the search for inner peace, and the quest for wisdom echo Boethian ideas. Writers use these themes to delve into the human condition, examining how individuals navigate the challenges and uncertainties of modern life.

Filmmakers also find inspiration in Boethius' work. Movies that tackle existential questions explore the nature of happiness, or depict characters grappling with their fate reflect Boethian themes. These films bring Boethius' ideas to a new audience, using the visual and narrative power of cinema to explore philosophical concepts.

In the realm of music, Boethius' influence can be seen in compositions that incorporate philosophical themes. Contemporary composers create works that reflect on the nature of fortune, the search for meaning, and the interplay of fate and free will. These musical compositions continue the tradition of exploring deep philosophical questions through the art of sound.

Visual artists, too, draw on Boethius' ideas in their work. Paintings, sculptures, and installations that explore themes of chance, destiny, and inner virtue reflect Boethian influence. These artworks engage viewers in a dialogue about the nature of existence, encouraging them to reflect on their own lives and experiences.

Boethius' influence in contemporary arts demonstrates the timeless relevance of his ideas. Artists across various mediums continue to find inspiration in his exploration of the human condition, creating works that resonate with modern audiences. The enduring appeal of Boethius' themes highlights their universal significance and their power to inspire creativity and reflection in the arts.

## CULTURAL REPRESENTATIONS

Boethius' work has been represented in various cultural forms over the centuries, reflecting the wide-ranging impact of his ideas. From literature and music to visual arts and theater, Boethius' themes and concepts have permeated many aspects of cultural expression. These representations highlight the enduring relevance and appeal of his work.

In literature, Boethius' influence can be seen in the works of many great authors. Geoffrey Chaucer, William Shakespeare, and Dante Alighieri all drew on Boethius' themes in their writings. These literary representations of Boethius' ideas have helped to keep his work alive and relevant across different historical periods.

Music has also been a powerful medium for expressing Boethian themes. Composers have created works inspired by "The Consolation of Philosophy," exploring ideas of fate, fortune, and the search for meaning through musical composition. These pieces reflect the emotional and intellectual depth of Boethius' work, bringing his ideas to life through sound.

Visual representations of Boethius' work are found in illuminated manuscripts, paintings, and sculptures. Medieval and Renaissance artists created beautiful depictions of scenes from "The Consolation of Philosophy," illustrating key moments and themes from the text. These visual representations have helped to convey the philosophical and emotional richness of Boethius' ideas.

Theater and performance have also played a role in representing Boethius' work. Dramatic adaptations of "The Consolation of Philosophy" bring the dialogue between Boethius and Lady Philosophy to life on stage. These performances engage audiences with the philosophical and existential questions posed by Boethius, making his ideas accessible and compelling.

Boethius' cultural representations demonstrate the wide-ranging impact of his work. His ideas have inspired artists across different mediums and historical periods, reflecting their timeless relevance. Through literature, music, visual arts, and theater, Boethius' themes continue to captivate and inspire, highlighting the enduring significance of his contributions to cultural and intellectual history.

# BOETHIUS' PHILOSOPHICAL METHODOLOGY

⁂

## DIALECTICAL REASONING

Boethius often used dialectical reasoning in his works. This method involves a dialogue between two or more people who hold different points of view. The goal is to explore these views and find the truth through reasoned argument. It's a back-and-forth conversation that helps to clarify ideas and resolve contradictions.

Dialectical reasoning is effective because it challenges assumptions and encourages critical thinking. Boethius used this method to delve deeply into philosophical questions. By presenting different perspectives, he could examine the strengths and weaknesses of each argument. This process allowed him to reach more nuanced and well-supported conclusions.

In "The Consolation of Philosophy," Boethius uses dialectical reasoning through his dialogue with Lady Philosophy. They discuss various topics, such as the nature of happiness and the role of fortune. Lady Philosophy guides Boethius through a series of questions and answers, helping him to see beyond his initial despair and confusion. This methodical approach helps Boethius find clarity and peace.

Dialectical reasoning also makes philosophy more accessible. Instead of presenting ideas as fixed truths, it shows them as part of an ongoing conversation. This invites readers to engage with the material and think for themselves. Boethius' use of this technique makes his work more dynamic and engaging.

Overall, dialectical reasoning is a key part of Boethius' philosophical methodology. It allows for a thorough exploration of complex ideas and promotes a deeper understanding. By using this method, Boethius encourages his readers to question, reflect, and seek the truth.


## USE OF CLASSICAL SOURCES

Boethius was deeply influenced by the works of classical philosophers. He drew extensively on the writings of Plato, Aristotle, and the Stoics. By integrating these sources into his own work, Boethius connected his ideas with a rich tradition of philosophical thought. This approach gave his arguments greater depth and credibility.

Plato's influence on Boethius is evident in his use of dialogues and his focus on the pursuit of the Good. Plato's emphasis on ideal forms and the importance of philosophical inquiry resonated with Boethius. He adopted Plato's method of exploring ideas through conversations between characters, which allowed for a more dynamic and engaging presentation of complex concepts.

BOETHIUS FOR BEGINNERS

Aristotle's impact is seen in Boethius' logical and analytical approach. Aristotle's works on logic, such as the "Organon," provided a framework for Boethius' own investigations. By applying Aristotle's principles of reasoning, Boethius was able to construct clear and compelling arguments. This logical rigor is a hallmark of his philosophical methodology.

The Stoics also influenced Boethius, particularly in their views on virtue and the nature of the cosmos. The Stoic belief in living according to nature and the importance of inner tranquility resonated with Boethius' own experiences. He incorporated these ideas into his discussions on happiness and the role of fortune, emphasizing the need for inner strength and resilience.

By using classical sources, Boethius demonstrated the continuity of philosophical thought. He showed that contemporary issues could be understood and addressed through the wisdom of the past. This connection to classical philosophy provided a solid foundation for his own ideas and helped to bridge the gap between ancient and medieval thought.

Boethius' use of classical sources enriched his work and made it more persuasive. By building on the ideas of Plato, Aristotle, and the Stoics, he created a comprehensive and well-rounded philosophical system. This approach not only honored the legacy of these great thinkers but also ensured that their insights continued to inform and inspire future generations.

PHILOSOPHICAL ARGUMENTATION

Boethius was skilled in the art of philosophical argumentation. He knew how to build strong, logical arguments and

85

how to anticipate and counter objections. His ability to argue effectively was a key part of his philosophical methodology. It allowed him to explore complex ideas thoroughly and convincingly.

One of Boethius' techniques was to start with clear definitions. He understood that a good argument begins with a clear understanding of the terms being used. By defining his concepts precisely, he set a solid foundation for his arguments. This clarity helped to avoid confusion and misinterpretation.

Boethius also used logical structure in his arguments. He would lay out his premises clearly and then show how they led to his conclusions. This step-by-step approach made his arguments easy to follow and hard to refute. By carefully constructing his reasoning, Boethius demonstrated the strength and validity of his ideas.

Another key aspect of Boethius' argumentation was his use of examples and analogies. He knew that abstract ideas could be difficult to grasp, so he used concrete examples to illustrate his points. Analogies helped to make his arguments more relatable and understandable. This technique also made his writing more engaging and persuasive.

Boethius was also adept at addressing counterarguments. He anticipated objections to his views and responded to them directly. By acknowledging and refuting these objections, he strengthened his own arguments. This thorough approach showed that he had considered multiple perspectives and that his conclusions were well-supported.

Philosophical argumentation was central to Boethius' methodology. His ability to build clear, logical arguments and to address counterarguments made his work rigorous and compelling. This skill in argumentation allowed Boethius to explore philosophical questions in depth and to communicate his ideas effectively.

## SOCRATIC DIALOGUE STYLE

Boethius often used the Socratic dialogue style in his writings. This method, named after the ancient Greek philosopher Socrates, involves a conversational approach to exploring ideas. By using dialogues, Boethius made his philosophical discussions more dynamic and engaging. This style also allowed him to present multiple perspectives and to explore the complexities of each issue.

In "The Consolation of Philosophy," Boethius uses a dialogue between himself and Lady Philosophy. This conversation format helps to break down complex ideas into more manageable parts. Lady Philosophy guides Boethius through a series of questions and answers, helping him to understand and resolve his doubts. This method encourages readers to think critically and to follow the logical progression of the discussion.

The Socratic dialogue style also emphasizes the importance of questioning. Boethius uses questions to challenge assumptions and to probe deeper into philosophical issues. This approach helps to uncover underlying beliefs and to clarify ideas. By asking the right questions, Boethius leads his readers to new insights and understanding.

Another benefit of the dialogue style is that it makes philosophy more accessible. Instead of presenting ideas in a dry, academic manner, Boethius uses conversations to illustrate his points. This makes his writing more relatable and engaging. Readers can see themselves in the characters and can follow the discussion as if they were part of it.

The use of dialogues also allows Boethius to present opposing viewpoints. By including different perspectives in the conversation, he can explore the strengths and weaknesses of each position. This balanced approach helps to provide a more comprehensive understanding of the issues at hand. It also shows that Boethius is open to considering multiple viewpoints and is committed to finding the truth.

Boethius' use of the Socratic dialogue style is a key part of his philosophical methodology. This approach makes his work more engaging, accessible, and thorough. By using dialogues, Boethius is able to explore complex ideas in a way that is both clear and compelling.

## CRITIQUE AND DEFENSE

Boethius was not only a philosopher who presented his own ideas but also one who critiqued the ideas of others. He believed that a thorough examination of different viewpoints was essential for discovering the truth. This critical approach was a key part of his philosophical methodology. Boethius' ability to critique and defend ideas made his work more rigorous and comprehensive.

One of the ways Boethius critiqued ideas was by identifying logical inconsistencies. He carefully examined the arguments of others, looking for any contradictions or weaknesses. By pointing out these flaws, he was able to challenge the validity of these ideas. This critical scrutiny helped to refine and improve philosophical discourse.

Boethius also used critique as a way to strengthen his own arguments. By considering potential objections to his views, he could address them directly and provide counterarguments. This proactive approach showed that he had thoroughly thought through his ideas and was prepared to defend them. It also demonstrated his commitment to intellectual honesty and rigor.

In addition to critiquing the ideas of others, Boethius defended his own positions with equal rigor. He provided clear and logical arguments to support his views, anticipating and responding to possible objections. This defensive strategy helped to reinforce the strength and validity of his ideas. By defending his positions effectively, Boethius demonstrated the robustness of his philosophical methodology.

Boethius' critical approach extended to both philosophical and theological ideas. He engaged with the works of ancient philosophers, such as Plato and Aristotle, as well as with contemporary theological debates. His critiques and defenses covered a wide range of topics, from the nature of happiness to the existence of God. This breadth of engagement highlighted his intellectual versatility and depth.

The critique and defense of ideas were central to Boethius' philosophical methodology. His ability to critically examine different viewpoints and to defend his own positions made his work more thorough and compelling. This approach ensured that his ideas were well-supported and that his contributions to philosophy were both rigorous and insightful.

## INTEGRATION OF LOGIC AND RHETORIC

Boethius was a master of integrating logic and rhetoric in his philosophical writings. He believed that effective communication of ideas required both clear reasoning and persuasive language. This integration of logic and rhetoric was a key aspect of his methodology, making his work both intellectually rigorous and engaging.

Logic was the foundation of Boethius' philosophical arguments. He used logical principles to construct clear and compelling arguments. By following the rules of logic, Boethius ensured that his conclusions were well-supported by evidence and reasoning. This logical rigor was essential for the credibility and strength of his ideas.

Rhetoric, on the other hand, was the art of persuasion. Boethius used rhetorical techniques to present his ideas in a way that was persuasive and appealing to his readers. He employed various rhetorical devices, such as analogies, metaphors, and vivid descriptions, to illustrate his points and to engage his audience. This rhetorical skill made his writing more dynamic and impactful.

The integration of logic and rhetoric allowed Boethius to communicate complex ideas effectively. By combining clear reasoning with persuasive language, he could make his arguments more accessible and compelling. This approach helped to bridge the gap between abstract philosophical concepts and the everyday experiences of his readers.

Boethius' use of rhetoric also enhanced the emotional appeal of his work. He knew that philosophy was not just about intellectual understanding but also about personal transformation. By using rhetorical techniques, Boethius was able to connect with his readers on an emotional level, inspiring them to reflect on their own lives and to seek wisdom and virtue.

The integration of logic and rhetoric in Boethius' work is a testament to his skill as a philosopher and a writer. This approach made his ideas more compelling and accessible, ensuring that his contributions to philosophy were both rigorous and engaging. Boethius' ability to combine logic and rhetoric remains a model for effective philosophical communication.

## BOETHIUS' METHOD IN CONTEXT

Boethius' philosophical methodology must be understood in the context of his time. He lived during a period of transition when the Roman Empire was falling and the medieval world was emerging. This historical context influenced his approach to philosophy and shaped his contributions to intellectual thought.

One of the key aspects of Boethius' context was the integration of classical and Christian traditions. He sought to harmonize the wisdom of ancient Greek and Roman philosophers with the teachings of Christianity. This synthesis was a defining feature of his methodology, reflecting the broader cultural and intellectual currents of his time.

Boethius' approach was also influenced by the educational practices of his era. He was trained in the liberal arts, which emphasized a broad and integrated approach to knowledge. This education provided him with a foundation in logic, rhetoric, mathematics, and philosophy, all of which informed his work. The interdisciplinary nature of his education is evident in his writings.

The political and social turmoil of Boethius' time also shaped his methodology. Faced with personal adversity and political instability, Boethius turned to philosophy as a source of solace and guidance. His works reflect a deep concern with questions of justice, virtue, and the role of fortune. This focus on practical and ethical issues made his philosophy relevant to the challenges of his time.

Boethius' methodology was also marked by a commitment to intellectual rigor and honesty. He believed that the search for truth required careful reasoning and a willingness to engage with different perspectives. This commitment is evident in his use of dialectical reasoning, critique, and defense. Boethius' method reflects a deep respect for the complexity of philosophical inquiry.

Understanding Boethius' method in context highlights the relevance and significance of his work. His approach to philosophy was shaped by the cultural, intellectual, and historical currents of his time. This context enriches our understanding of Boethius' contributions and underscores the enduring impact of his methodology on Western thought.

# THE RECEPTION OF BOETHIUS
## IN MODERN PHILOSOPHY

## ENLIGHTENMENT THINKERS

During the Enlightenment, Boethius was seen as a bridge between the ancient and modern worlds. Enlightenment thinkers admired his ability to blend classical philosophy with early Christian thought. They appreciated his logical rigor and his commitment to reason. Boethius' works were studied and respected by many intellectuals of the time.

One Enlightenment philosopher who was influenced by Boethius was Voltaire. Voltaire admired Boethius' ability to find meaning and comfort in philosophy during his imprisonment. He saw Boethius as a model of how reason and intellect could provide solace in times of distress. Voltaire's own writings often reflected this admiration for Boethius' approach to life's challenges.

Another Enlightenment figure who engaged with Boethius' ideas was Immanuel Kant. Kant was interested in the way

Boethius reconciled faith and reason. He saw Boethius as a precursor to his own attempts to understand the relationship between knowledge and belief. Kant's philosophy of critical inquiry owes much to the groundwork laid by Boethius.

Boethius also influenced Enlightenment discussions on ethics and morality. His emphasis on inner virtue and the pursuit of the good life resonated with thinkers like John Locke and David Hume. They appreciated Boethius' exploration of happiness and the role of fortune, which informed their own ideas about human well-being and justice.

The reception of Boethius during the Enlightenment highlights his enduring relevance. His ability to integrate different philosophical traditions and his commitment to rational inquiry made him a valuable figure for Enlightenment thinkers. Boethius' work provided a foundation for the intellectual explorations of this era, demonstrating the timeless appeal of his ideas.

## 19TH CENTURY PHILOSOPHICAL DEBATES

In the 19th century, Boethius' ideas continued to be a topic of interest among philosophers. This period saw intense debates about the nature of knowledge, ethics, and the role of religion in society. Boethius' works were revisited and reinterpreted in light of these discussions, showing their ongoing relevance.

One key figure in 19th-century philosophy who engaged with Boethius' ideas was Friedrich Nietzsche. Nietzsche was critical of many aspects of traditional philosophy, but he found value in Boethius' emphasis on inner strength and resilience. Nietzsche's concept of the "will to power" echoes

Boethius' idea that true happiness comes from within rather than from external circumstances.

John Stuart Mill, another prominent philosopher of the 19th century, also engaged with Boethian themes. Mill's utilitarian ethics emphasized the greatest happiness principle, which aligns with Boethius' focus on the pursuit of the good life. Mill admired Boethius' exploration of the nature of happiness and the importance of virtue.

The 19th century also saw a renewed interest in medieval philosophy, including the works of Boethius. Scholars and philosophers began to recognize the value of medieval thought in shaping modern ideas. Boethius' integration of classical and Christian philosophy was seen as a precursor to many modern philosophical debates about faith, reason, and ethics.

Boethius' influence can also be seen in the works of Søren Kierkegaard. Kierkegaard, often considered the father of existentialism, was deeply concerned with the nature of existence and the human condition. Boethius' reflections on suffering, fate, and the search for meaning resonated with Kierkegaard's own philosophical inquiries.

The 19th century was a period of intense philosophical exploration and debate. Boethius' ideas provided valuable insights and perspectives for many of these discussions. His work continued to inspire and challenge philosophers, demonstrating its enduring significance in the evolving landscape of modern thought.

## 20TH CENTURY REINTERPRETATIONS

In the 20th century, Boethius' work was reinterpreted in various ways. Philosophers and scholars examined his ideas through new lenses, incorporating insights from contemporary thought. This period saw a resurgence of interest in medieval philosophy, with Boethius' work receiving significant attention.

One major figure in 20th-century philosophy who engaged with Boethius was Ludwig Wittgenstein. Wittgenstein's exploration of language and meaning resonated with Boethius' own reflections on the nature of reality and knowledge. Wittgenstein's later work, which focused on the use of language in everyday life, echoed Boethius' emphasis on practical wisdom and the lived experience of philosophy.

Existentialist philosophers like Jean-Paul Sartre and Martin Heidegger also found inspiration in Boethius. Sartre's exploration of freedom and the human condition reflected themes present in Boethius' writings. Heidegger's focus on being and time can be seen as a continuation of Boethius' inquiries into the nature of existence and the role of fate and providence.

The 20th century also saw the development of new methodologies for studying medieval philosophy. Scholars used historical and philological approaches to gain a deeper understanding of Boethius' work and its context. This led to a renewed appreciation of Boethius as a pivotal figure in the history of philosophy, bridging the ancient and medieval worlds.

Boethius' ideas were also explored in the context of modern ethical theory. Philosophers like Alasdair MacIntyre revisited Boethius' concepts of virtue and the good life. MacIntyre's work on virtue ethics drew on Boethius' insights, emphasizing the importance of moral character and the role of community in ethical development.

The reinterpretations of Boethius' work in the 20th century highlight its ongoing relevance. Philosophers and scholars continued to find new ways to engage with his ideas, demonstrating their adaptability and depth. Boethius' work remained a vital source of inspiration and insight, influencing a wide range of philosophical discussions.

## BOETHIUS AND EXISTENTIALISM

Boethius' work has had a significant impact on existentialist thought. Existentialism, which emerged in the 20th century, focuses on the nature of existence, freedom, and the human condition. Many of Boethius' themes resonate with existentialist concerns, making his work relevant to this philosophical movement.

One of the key existentialist themes in Boethius' work is the search for meaning. In "The Consolation of Philosophy," Boethius grapples with questions of fate, suffering, and the pursuit of happiness. These issues are central to existentialist philosophy, which seeks to understand how individuals can find meaning in an often chaotic and indifferent world.

Existentialist philosophers like Jean-Paul Sartre and Albert Camus explored similar themes in their writings. Sartre's concept of "bad faith" and Camus' notion of "the absurd" reflect the existential struggle to find meaning and authenticity in life. Boethius' reflections on the nature of happiness and the role of inner virtue offer valuable insights into this existential quest.

Boethius' emphasis on the importance of personal responsibility and inner strength also aligns with existentialist ideas. Existentialists believe that individuals must take responsibility for their own lives and create their own meaning. Boethius' focus on cultivating inner virtues and finding happiness within oneself echoes this existentialist emphasis on personal agency.

The theme of freedom is another area of convergence between Boethius and existentialism. Existentialists explore the concept of freedom as both a possibility and a burden. Boethius' discussions on the nature of free will and its relationship to divine providence offer a philosophical framework for understanding the complexities of human freedom.

Boethius' influence on existentialism demonstrates the enduring relevance of his work. His exploration of fundamental questions about existence, meaning, and freedom resonates with existentialist concerns. Boethius' insights continue to inspire and inform existentialist thought, highlighting the timeless significance of his philosophical contributions.

## CONTEMPORARY ANALYSES

In contemporary philosophy, Boethius' work continues to be analyzed and explored. Modern scholars and philosophers examine his ideas through various theoretical lenses, incorporating insights from current philosophical trends. This ongoing engagement with Boethius' work highlights its relevance to contemporary thought.

One area of contemporary analysis is the intersection of Boethius' ideas with modern ethical theory. Philosophers like Martha Nussbaum and Charles Taylor have explored Boethius' concepts of virtue and the good life. They examine how Boethius' insights can inform contemporary discussions on ethics, morality, and human flourishing.

Another area of interest is the relationship between Boethius' work and contemporary metaphysics. Scholars analyze Boethius' ideas about the nature of reality, time, and existence. They explore how his reflections on these topics can contribute to modern debates in metaphysics and ontology. Boethius' work offers a rich source of philosophical inquiry in these areas.

Boethius' contributions to logic and philosophy of language are also subjects of contemporary analysis. Philosophers examine his logical theories and their relevance to modern discussions on language, meaning, and argumentation. Boethius' integration of logic and rhetoric provides valuable insights for understanding the relationship between language and thought.

Contemporary philosophers also explore Boethius' impact on political philosophy. His reflections on justice, power, and the role of the individual in society resonate with current debates on political ethics and governance. Boethius' ideas offer a historical perspective that enriches contemporary discussions on these topics.

The ongoing analysis of Boethius' work in contemporary philosophy demonstrates its lasting significance. His ideas continue to inspire and inform a wide range of philosophical discussions. Boethius' work remains a vital source of insight and inspiration for modern scholars and thinkers.

## BOETHIUS IN MODERN ETHICAL THOUGHT

Boethius' ideas have had a profound impact on modern ethical thought. His emphasis on inner virtue and the pursuit of the good life resonates with contemporary discussions on ethics and morality. Modern philosophers and ethicists draw on Boethius' insights to explore the nature of happiness, virtue, and moral character.

One of the key contributions of Boethius to modern ethical thought is his concept of happiness. Boethius argues that true happiness is found within, through the cultivation of virtue and wisdom. This idea aligns with modern approaches to well-being and flourishing, which emphasize the importance of inner fulfillment and moral integrity.

Boethius' focus on virtue ethics has also influenced contemporary ethical theory. Philosophers like Alasdair MacIntyre have built on Boethius' ideas to develop a modern understanding of virtue ethics. This approach emphasizes the importance of moral character and the role of community in ethical development. Boethius' insights provide a historical foundation for these contemporary discussions.

The role of fortune and external circumstances in ethical life is another area where Boethius' ideas are relevant. Boethius explores how individuals can maintain their virtue and happiness despite the ups and downs of fortune. This theme is important in modern ethical thought, which examines how people can live morally and meaningfully in the face of adversity.

Boethius' reflections on justice and the common good also contribute to modern ethical discussions. He argues that true justice is grounded in the pursuit of the common good and the cultivation of virtue. This perspective aligns with contemporary debates on social justice and the ethical responsibilities of individuals and institutions.

Boethius' impact on modern ethical thought highlights the timeless relevance of his ideas. His emphasis on virtue, happiness, and justice continues to inspire and inform contemporary ethical theory. Boethius' work provides valuable insights for understanding and addressing the ethical challenges of the modern world.

## FUTURE DIRECTIONS IN BOETHIAN STUDIES

As interest in Boethius' work continues to grow, scholars are exploring new directions in Boethian studies. These future directions promise to deepen our understanding of Boethius' ideas and their relevance to contemporary thought. They also highlight the ongoing significance of Boethius' work in the history of philosophy.

One promising direction is the interdisciplinary study of Boethius' work. Scholars are examining how Boethius' ideas intersect with fields like literature, music, and the visual arts. This interdisciplinary approach provides a more comprehensive understanding of Boethius' influence and demonstrates the breadth of his impact on Western culture.

Another area of interest is the exploration of Boethius' contributions to the philosophy of religion. Scholars are examining his reflections on faith, reason, and the nature of God in light of contemporary religious thought. This research offers new insights into Boethius' theological ideas and their relevance to modern discussions on religion and spirituality.

The study of Boethius' impact on medieval and Renaissance thought is also a growing field. Researchers are uncovering new connections between Boethius and later philosophers, demonstrating how his ideas shaped intellectual developments in these periods. This historical approach provides a richer context for understanding Boethius' work and its legacy.

Scholars are also exploring the reception of Boethius' work in non-Western philosophical traditions. By examining how Boethius' ideas have been interpreted and adapted in different cultural contexts, researchers are broadening the scope of Boethian studies. This global perspective enriches our understanding of Boethius' contributions to philosophy.

The future of Boethian studies promises to be an exciting and dynamic field. As scholars continue to explore new directions and interdisciplinary approaches, our understanding of Boethius' work will deepen and expand. Boethius' ideas will continue to inspire and inform, demonstrating their enduring relevance and significance in the history of philosophy.

# PRACTICAL APPLICATIONS OF
# BOETHIAN PHILOSOPHY

## ETHICS IN DAILY LIFE

Boethius' philosophy isn't just for scholars; it offers practical advice for everyday living. One of his key ideas is that true happiness comes from within, not from external goods. This means that people should focus on developing their character and inner virtues rather than chasing material success. This perspective encourages a more thoughtful and meaningful approach to life.

In daily life, Boethius' emphasis on inner virtues can guide our actions and decisions. For example, when faced with a moral dilemma, we can ask ourselves what the virtuous choice would be. By focusing on honesty, kindness, and justice, we can make decisions that align with our core values. This approach not only helps us act ethically but also fosters personal integrity and self-respect.

Boethius also teaches us to maintain perspective in the face of life's ups and downs. By understanding that fortune is fickle and external circumstances can change rapidly, we can remain grounded. This mindset helps us appreciate the good times without becoming overly attached to them and endure difficult times without losing hope. It's a balanced way to navigate the unpredictability of life.

Furthermore, Boethius' ideas encourage us to look beyond immediate gratification. In a world that often emphasizes quick rewards, his philosophy reminds us of the importance of long-term fulfillment. By cultivating patience and perseverance, we can work towards goals that bring deeper and more lasting satisfaction. This approach is particularly relevant in today's fast-paced society.

Applying Boethius' philosophy to daily life means striving to live with purpose and integrity. It involves making conscious choices that reflect our values and staying resilient in the face of challenges. By focusing on inner virtues and long-term fulfillment, we can lead more meaningful and satisfying lives.

## RESILIENCE AND ADVERSITY

Boethius knew a lot about adversity. He wrote "The Consolation of Philosophy" while he was in prison, awaiting execution. Despite his dire situation, he found a way to maintain hope and resilience. His philosophy teaches us how to stay strong in the face of adversity, which is a valuable lesson for anyone dealing with difficulties.

Boethius also emphasized the importance of perspective. He encouraged looking at the bigger picture and understanding that challenges are a part of life. This mindset helps us see that difficulties are temporary and can often lead to personal growth. By adopting a broader perspective, we can find meaning in our struggles and use them as opportunities for development.

Another aspect of resilience is acceptance. Boethius taught that we should accept what we cannot change and focus on what we can control. This doesn't mean giving up but rather redirecting our energy toward productive and positive actions. Acceptance helps us avoid wasting energy on things beyond our control and allows us to focus on our strengths and capabilities.

Lastly, Boethius believed in the power of reflection and self-awareness. By regularly reflecting on our experiences and emotions, we can gain insights into our behavior and attitudes. This practice helps us learn from our challenges and build resilience over time. It encourages a proactive approach to personal growth and self-improvement.

Boethius' teachings on resilience and adversity are highly relevant today. They provide practical strategies for staying strong in the face of challenges and finding meaning in difficult situations. By focusing on inner virtues, maintaining perspective, practicing acceptance, and reflecting on our experiences, we can build resilience and thrive despite adversity.

## PHILOSOPHICAL COUNSELING

Philosophical counseling is an approach to therapy that uses philosophical concepts to help people navigate life's challenges. Boethius' philosophy is particularly well-suited for this purpose. His ideas about happiness, virtue, and resilience offer valuable insights for those seeking guidance and support. Philosophical counseling can help individuals find clarity and purpose by applying Boethian principles.

One key aspect of philosophical counseling is helping clients understand the nature of true happiness. Boethius taught that genuine happiness comes from within through the cultivation of virtue. Counselors can use this idea to guide clients in exploring their values and developing a sense of inner fulfillment. This approach helps individuals focus on long-term well-being rather than fleeting pleasures.

Another important concept in Boethian philosophy is the role of fortune and adversity. Philosophical counselors can help clients recognize that external circumstances are often beyond their control. By focusing on their inner strengths and virtues, clients can build resilience and maintain hope in difficult times. This perspective encourages a proactive and empowered approach to life's challenges.

Philosophical counseling also involves exploring ethical decision-making. Boethius believed that living a virtuous life leads to true happiness. Counselors can help clients reflect on their choices and actions, encouraging them to align their behavior with their core values. This process fosters personal integrity and helps clients develop a stronger sense of purpose and direction.

Self-reflection is another key element of philosophical counseling. Boethius emphasized the importance of understanding oneself and one's emotions. Counselors can guide clients in developing self-awareness and reflective practices. This helps individuals gain insights into their thoughts and behaviors, leading to personal growth and improved emotional well-being.

Boethian principles in philosophical counseling provide a holistic approach to personal development and well-being. By focusing on inner virtues, resilience, ethical decision-making, and self-reflection, individuals can find greater clarity and purpose in their lives. Philosophical counseling offers a valuable framework for navigating life's challenges and achieving lasting fulfillment.

## MORAL DECISION MAKING

Boethius' philosophy offers valuable guidance for moral decision-making. His emphasis on inner virtue and the pursuit of the good life provides a framework for making ethical choices. By focusing on what is morally right rather than what is convenient or beneficial in the short term, Boethius' teachings help individuals navigate complex moral dilemmas.

One of Boethius' key principles is that true happiness comes from living a virtuous life. This means that moral decisions should be guided by virtues such as honesty, justice, and kindness. When faced with a difficult choice, individuals can ask themselves what the virtuous action would be. This approach encourages ethical behavior and personal integrity.

Boethius also believed in the importance of intention in moral decision-making. He taught that the motives behind our actions are just as important as the actions themselves. This means that individuals should reflect on their reasons for making a particular choice and ensure that their intentions align with their values. This focus on intention helps to ensure that actions are genuinely ethical.

Another important aspect of Boethian moral decision-making is considering the long-term consequences of actions. Boethius emphasized the pursuit of the good life, which involves thinking about how decisions will impact one's overall well-being and the well-being of others. This perspective encourages individuals to consider the broader implications of their choices and to act in ways that promote lasting happiness and fulfillment.

Boethius' philosophy also highlights the importance of personal responsibility in moral decision-making. He believed that individuals have the power to choose their actions and should be held accountable for their decisions. This means that individuals should take ownership of their choices and be prepared to accept the consequences. This sense of responsibility fosters ethical behavior and personal growth.

Incorporating Boethian principles into moral decision-making provides a clear and practical framework for navigating ethical dilemmas. By focusing on virtue, intention, long-term consequences, and personal responsibility, individuals can make decisions that align with their values and promote a meaningful and fulfilling life.

## PERSONAL GROWTH AND VIRTUE

Boethius' philosophy places a strong emphasis on personal growth and the cultivation of virtue. He believed that true happiness comes from developing one's character and living a life of moral integrity. This focus on personal growth and virtue provides valuable insights for those seeking to improve themselves and lead more meaningful lives.

One of Boethius' key teachings is the importance of self-awareness in personal growth. He believed that individuals should regularly reflect on their thoughts, emotions, and behaviors. This self-reflection helps individuals gain insights into their strengths and weaknesses, allowing them to make conscious efforts to improve. By understanding themselves better, individuals can work towards becoming the best versions of themselves.

Boethius also emphasized the role of virtue in personal growth. He believed that cultivating virtues such as honesty, courage, and compassion is essential for achieving true happiness. Individuals can focus on developing these virtues through deliberate practice and effort. By striving to embody these qualities in their daily lives, they can build a strong moral character and find greater fulfillment.

Another important aspect of Boethian personal growth is the idea of resilience. Boethius taught that individuals should cultivate inner strength and resilience to navigate life's challenges. This involves developing a positive mindset, practicing self-discipline, and maintaining a sense of purpose. Resilience helps individuals stay grounded and focused, even in the face of adversity.

Boethius also believed in the importance of lifelong learning and growth. He encouraged individuals to seek knowledge and wisdom throughout their lives. This pursuit of learning helps individuals expand their horizons and deepen their understanding of the world. It also fosters a sense of curiosity and openness, which are essential for personal development.

Personal growth and virtue, according to Boethius, are key to achieving a meaningful and fulfilling life. By focusing on self-awareness, cultivating virtues, building resilience, and seeking lifelong learning, individuals can grow and thrive. Boethius' philosophy offers valuable guidance for those seeking to improve themselves and lead a life of moral integrity.

## MODERN THERAPEUTIC USES

Boethius' philosophy has found applications in modern therapy and counseling. His insights into happiness, resilience, and virtue offer valuable tools for helping individuals navigate life's challenges and improve their well-being. Therapists and counselors can draw on Boethian principles to support their clients in meaningful and effective ways.

One therapeutic application of Boethius' philosophy is in cognitive-behavioral therapy (CBT). CBT focuses on changing negative thought patterns and behaviors to improve mental health. Boethius' emphasis on inner virtues and positive mindset aligns well with this approach. Therapists can use Boethian ideas to help clients develop healthier thinking patterns and cultivate inner strength.

Boethius' teachings on resilience are also relevant in therapy. His philosophy encourages individuals to find strength within themselves and to maintain hope in difficult times. Therapists can help clients build resilience by exploring Boethian principles of acceptance, perspective, and inner virtue. This approach can support clients in developing the skills needed to cope with adversity.

Another modern therapeutic use of Boethius' philosophy is in existential therapy. This form of therapy focuses on exploring the meaning and purpose of life. Boethius' reflections on happiness, fate, and the search for meaning provide a rich framework for existential exploration. Therapists can use Boethian concepts to guide clients in understanding their experiences and finding a sense of purpose.

Boethius' philosophy also offers insights for mindfulness-based therapies. His emphasis on self-awareness and reflection aligns with the principles of mindfulness. Therapists can incorporate Boethian practices of self-reflection and contemplation into their sessions, helping clients develop greater self-awareness and emotional regulation.

Overall, Boethius' philosophy provides valuable tools for modern therapeutic practices. His insights into happiness, resilience, and virtue offer practical strategies for improving mental health and well-being. By incorporating Boethian principles into therapy, counselors can support their clients in meaningful and effective ways.

BOETHIUS' WISDOM TODAY

Boethius' philosophy remains relevant and valuable in today's world. His insights into happiness, virtue, and resilience offer timeless wisdom that can guide individuals in leading meaningful and fulfilling lives. By applying Boethian principles, people can navigate the complexities of modern life with greater clarity and purpose.

One key aspect of Boethius' wisdom is his emphasis on inner happiness. In a world that often emphasizes material success and external achievements, Boethius reminds us that true happiness comes from within. By focusing on developing our inner virtues and cultivating a positive mindset, we can find lasting fulfillment regardless of our external circumstances.

Boethius' teachings on resilience are also highly relevant today. Life is full of challenges and uncertainties, and Boethius' philosophy offers practical strategies for staying strong in the face of adversity. By practicing acceptance, maintaining perspective, and focusing on our inner strengths, we can build resilience and navigate life's ups and downs with grace.

Boethius' reflections on virtue provide valuable guidance for ethical living. In a time when ethical dilemmas and moral complexities are common, his emphasis on honesty, kindness, and justice can help us make better decisions. By striving to live a virtuous life, we can contribute to a more just and compassionate society.

The relevance of Boethius' wisdom extends to personal growth and self-improvement. His philosophy encourages lifelong learning and self-reflection, which are essential for personal development. By regularly reflecting on our experiences and seeking to improve ourselves, we can grow and thrive in all aspects of life.

Boethius' wisdom offers timeless guidance for leading a meaningful and fulfilling life. His emphasis on inner happiness, resilience, virtue, and personal growth provides practical strategies for navigating the complexities of modern life. By applying Boethian principles, we can find greater clarity, purpose, and fulfillment in our daily lives.

# CRITICISMS AND CONTROVERSIES

☙

## PHILOSOPHICAL CRITIQUES

Boethius' works have received their fair share of criticism over the centuries. Philosophers have pointed out several areas where they believe his ideas fall short. One major critique is that Boethius' blending of Christian theology with classical philosophy can sometimes feel forced. Critics argue that trying to merge these two distinct traditions results in inconsistencies and contradictions.

Another philosophical critique concerns Boethius' views on happiness and fortune. Some philosophers believe that his emphasis on inner virtue as the sole source of happiness overlooks the importance of external circumstances. They argue that while inner virtues are crucial, external factors such as health, relationships, and social conditions also significantly impact one's happiness.

Boethius' concept of divine providence has also been questioned. Critics argue that his explanation of how free will can coexist with a predetermined divine plan is not entirely convincing. They point out that Boethius' attempt to reconcile these two ideas leaves many questions unanswered and fails to fully address the complexities involved.

Furthermore, Boethius' reliance on Platonic and Aristotelian thought has been scrutinized. Some modern philosophers feel that his heavy dependence on these ancient thinkers limits the originality of his work. They argue that Boethius' ideas, while valuable, do not offer much that is new or groundbreaking but rather repackages existing philosophies in a Christian framework.

Despite these critiques, Boethius' work continues to be studied and respected. His ability to synthesize different philosophical traditions and his exploration of deep existential questions have left a lasting impact. While his ideas are not without flaws, they remain a significant contribution to the history of philosophy.

## HISTORICAL MISINTERPRETATIONS

Over time, Boethius' works have been subject to various interpretations and misinterpretations. One common historical misinterpretation involves the nature of his imprisonment and execution. Some historians have depicted Boethius as a purely political martyr, while others have focused solely on his philosophical contributions, neglecting the political context of his downfall.

Another historical misinterpretation concerns Boethius' identity. Some have portrayed him as primarily a Christian theologian, overshadowing his role as a philosopher who engaged deeply with pagan classical texts. This has led to an incomplete understanding of his efforts to bridge the gap between classical philosophy and Christian theology.

Misinterpretations have also arisen regarding Boethius' intentions in writing "The Consolation of Philosophy." Some have read it purely as a work of personal reflection and solace, ignoring its broader philosophical arguments. Others have interpreted it strictly as a philosophical text, over-looking its personal and emotional dimensions.

Additionally, translations of Boethius' works have sometimes introduced errors and biases. Translators' interpretations can influence how Boethius is understood by subsequent generations. These translation issues have occasionally led to misunderstandings of his key concepts and arguments.

Understanding these historical misinterpretations helps to clarify Boethius' true contributions. By recognizing the nuances of his work and the context in which he wrote, we can gain a more accurate and comprehensive view of his legacy. This involves appreciating both his philosophical insights and his personal experiences.

THEOLOGICAL DISPUTES

Boethius' attempts to integrate classical philosophy with Christian theology have sparked considerable theological disputes. One major area of contention is his concept of the nature of God. Boethius described God as both omnipotent and benevolent, but some theologians argue that this dual nature is difficult to reconcile with the existence of evil in the world.

Another theological dispute centers on Boethius' views on the Trinity. His explanations in "De Trinitate" aimed to clarify the relationship between the Father, Son, and Holy Spirit using philosophical reasoning. However, some theologians feel that his approach is too influenced by Greek philosophy and does not fully align with orthodox Christian teachings.

Boethius' ideas about predestination and free will have also been debated. He tried to explain how humans can have free will if God already knows everything that will happen. Some theologians argue that his explanation is inadequate and fails to fully resolve the tension between divine foreknowledge and human freedom.

His views on the nature of happiness and virtue have been another point of theological contention. Boethius argued that true happiness comes from within and is achieved through the cultivation of virtue. While many theologians agree with this, some believe that Boethius underemphasizes the role of God's grace in achieving true happiness.

These theological disputes highlight the complexity of Boethius' thought and its reception in the Christian tradition. While his efforts to reconcile faith and reason were groundbreaking, they also opened up debates that continue to this day. Understanding these disputes helps to appreciate the depth and impact of Boethius' work in theological circles.

## MODERN ACADEMIC DEBATES

In modern academia, Boethius' work continues to be a subject of intense debate. Scholars examine his contributions from various angles, including philosophy, theology, and literature. One major area of debate is the originality of Boethius' ideas. Some academics argue that he mainly transmitted existing philosophies rather than developing new ones, while others see him as a creative thinker who made significant contributions by synthesizing different traditions.

Another academic debate focuses on the interpretation of "The Consolation of Philosophy." Scholars discuss whether it should be read primarily as a philosophical treatise, a literary work, or a personal reflection. This debate influences how Boethius is taught in universities and how his work is understood in different academic disciplines.

Boethius' influence on medieval thought is also a topic of scholarly interest. Researchers explore how his works were received and interpreted by medieval philosophers and theologians. They examine the ways in which Boethius' ideas were incorporated into the broader intellectual landscape of the Middle Ages, including their impact on figures like Thomas Aquinas and Dante Alighieri.

Additionally, modern scholars debate the relevance of Boethius' ideas in contemporary philosophy. Some argue that his concepts of happiness, virtue, and resilience are timeless and applicable to modern life. Others believe that his ideas are too rooted in ancient and medieval contexts to be fully relevant today. This debate reflects broader discussions about the value of classical and medieval philosophy in the modern world.

These modern academic debates highlight the ongoing interest in Boethius' work. They show that his ideas continue to provoke thought and discussion, demonstrating their enduring significance. Engaging with these debates helps to keep Boethius' legacy alive and relevant in contemporary scholarship.

## CRITICISM OF BOETHIUS' METHODS

Boethius' methods have faced criticism from various quarters. One major critique is his heavy reliance on classical sources. Critics argue that Boethius' dependence on Plato and Aristotle sometimes limits his originality. They believe that he could have developed more innovative ideas had he relied less on these ancient philosophers.

Another criticism concerns Boethius' use of dialogue in "The Consolation of Philosophy." While the dialogue format can make complex ideas more accessible, some critics argue that it also leads to a lack of clarity and precision. They believe that the conversational style sometimes obscures Boethius' main arguments and makes it difficult to follow his line of reasoning.

Boethius' integration of philosophy and theology has also been critiqued. Some argue that his attempts to reconcile these two disciplines result in inconsistencies. They believe that Boethius' philosophical methods sometimes conflict with his theological commitments, leading to contradictions in his work.

Critics have also pointed out that Boethius' focus on inner virtue and resilience can be seen as overly individualistic. They argue that his emphasis on personal strength and virtue may neglect the importance of social and political factors in achieving happiness and justice. This perspective suggests that Boethius' methods may not fully address the complexities of human life.

Despite these criticisms, Boethius' methods have also been praised for their depth and rigor. His ability to synthesize different traditions and explore complex ideas in a clear and engaging way remains influential. While his methods may have limitations, they continue to offer valuable insights and provoke thoughtful discussion.

## CONTROVERSIES IN TRANSLATION

The translation of Boethius' works has been a source of controversy over the centuries. Different translators have interpreted his texts in various ways, sometimes leading to significant differences in meaning. These translation issues have affected how Boethius' ideas are understood and appreciated.

One major controversy concerns the translation of key philosophical terms. For example, the Latin word "felicitas" can be translated as "happiness" or "blessedness," depending on the context. Different translators' choices can influence how readers understand Boethius' concepts of happiness and virtue. This variability highlights the challenges of accurately conveying philosophical ideas across languages.

Another issue is the translation of Boethius' dialogues. The conversational style of "The Consolation of Philosophy" can be difficult to capture in other languages. Some translations may prioritize readability, while others aim for literal accuracy. These different approaches can result in varied interpretations of Boethius' arguments and ideas.

Historical context also plays a role in translation controversies. Early translations of Boethius' works were influenced by the cultural and intellectual climates of their times. For example, medieval translators might emphasize the theological aspects of his work, while Renaissance translators might focus on his classical influences. These contextual differences affect how Boethius is presented and understood.

Additionally, the translation of Boethius' poetry poses unique challenges. His use of meter, rhyme, and other poetic devices can be difficult to replicate in other languages. Translators must balance the need to preserve the poetic qualities of the text with the need to convey its philosophical content accurately. This balancing act can lead to different interpretations and emphases.

Understanding these translation controversies helps to appreciate the complexity of Boethius' work and its reception. It highlights the importance of careful and thoughtful translation in preserving the integrity of philosophical texts. Despite these challenges, the ongoing effort to translate Boethius' works ensures that his ideas remain accessible to new generations of readers.

## EVALUATING BOETHIUS' RELEVANCE

Evaluating Boethius' relevance today involves considering both the strengths and limitations of his ideas. On one hand, his emphasis on inner virtues and personal resilience remains highly applicable. In a world where external circumstances are often beyond our control, Boethius' focus on cultivating inner strength and wisdom offers valuable guidance.

Boethius' exploration of happiness and virtue also continues to resonate. His belief that true happiness comes from within and is achieved through the cultivation of virtue aligns with modern approaches to well-being and personal development. This perspective encourages individuals to focus on long-term fulfillment rather than fleeting pleasures.

However, some aspects of Boethius' work may seem less relevant in today's context. His heavy reliance on classical philosophy and Christian theology might not fully resonate with those who do not share these traditions. Additionally, his views on fortune and providence may be seen as overly deterministic, overlooking the complexities of free will and personal agency.

Modern scholars also debate the practical applicability of Boethius' ideas. While his philosophical insights are valuable, some argue that they may not fully address the social and political dimensions of contemporary life. Boethius' focus on individual virtue and resilience may need to be complemented by a broader consideration of systemic and structural issues.

Despite these debates, Boethius' work continues to offer timeless wisdom. His insights into the human condition, the nature of happiness, and the importance of virtue provide a rich source of guidance for navigating life's challenges. By engaging with Boethius' ideas, we can gain a deeper understanding of ourselves and the world around us.

Evaluating Boethius' relevance involves balancing the enduring strengths of his philosophy with an awareness of its limitations. His work offers valuable insights that can inspire and inform our lives, even as we adapt and reinterpret his ideas in light of contemporary realities. Boethius' legacy remains a testament to the enduring power of philosophical inquiry.

# CONCLUSION

## SUMMARY OF BOETHIUS' CONTRIBUTIONS

Boethius made many significant contributions to philosophy, literature, and theology. His most famous work, "The Consolation of Philosophy," combines deep philosophical inquiry with personal reflection. In it, Boethius tackles big questions about fate, happiness, and virtue while grappling with his own misfortunes. This unique blend of the personal and the philosophical has made his work timeless.

Beyond "The Consolation of Philosophy," Boethius also played a crucial role in preserving and transmitting classical knowledge. He translated many important works of Aristotle and Plato into Latin, making them accessible to the medieval world. These translations laid the foundation for much of medieval philosophy and helped bridge the gap between ancient and medieval thought.

Boethius' integration of classical philosophy with Christian theology is another key contribution. He worked to show

how the wisdom of the ancients could be harmonized with Christian beliefs. This synthesis of ideas influenced many later thinkers and helped shape the intellectual landscape of the Middle Ages.

His writings on logic and music theory were also influential. Boethius' logical works were used as textbooks for centuries, and his treatises on music helped establish the mathematical and philosophical foundations of medieval music theory. These contributions highlight his diverse intellectual interests and his ability to apply philosophical reasoning to a wide range of subjects.

Overall, Boethius' work has had a lasting impact on Western thought. His efforts to preserve classical knowledge, his philosophical inquiries, and his integration of different traditions have left a rich legacy. Boethius' contributions continue to be studied and appreciated for their depth, insight, and relevance.

## ENDURING PHILOSOPHICAL QUESTIONS

Boethius addressed many philosophical questions that remain relevant today. One of the most enduring is the nature of happiness. Boethius argued that true happiness comes from within and is achieved through the cultivation of virtue. This idea challenges us to think about what it means to live a good life and where we should seek fulfillment.

Another enduring question is the problem of evil. Boethius grappled with the question of why bad things happen to good people. His reflections on fate, fortune, and divine providence offer a way to think about suffering and adversity. These ideas continue to resonate with anyone who has faced hardships and sought to understand them.

Boethius also explored the relationship between free will and divine foreknowledge. He asked how humans can have free will if God already knows everything that will happen. This question remains a central issue in both philosophy and theology, as it touches on the nature of human freedom and the concept of destiny.

The nature of knowledge and understanding is another key question Boethius addressed. He believed in the importance of integrating reason and faith, arguing that true knowledge involves both philosophical inquiry and religious belief. This perspective encourages us to consider how different ways of knowing can complement each other.

Lastly, Boethius' work prompts us to think about the role of philosophy in our lives. He viewed philosophy as a source of solace and guidance, capable of helping us navigate life's challenges. This idea invites us to reflect on how philosophical thinking can enrich our personal and intellectual lives.

Boethius' exploration of these enduring questions highlights the timeless relevance of his work. His insights continue to inspire and challenge us, encouraging deeper reflection on the fundamental issues of human existence.

## BOETHIUS' RELEVANCE TO MODERN THOUGHT

Boethius' ideas remain relevant to modern thought in many ways. His emphasis on inner virtues and personal resilience is particularly applicable in today's fast-paced and often uncertain world. Boethius reminds us that true happiness and fulfillment come from within, not from external circumstances. This perspective encourages us to focus on developing our character and inner strengths.

His reflections on the nature of happiness offer valuable insights for contemporary discussions on well-being. In an age where people often seek quick fixes and instant gratification, Boethius' idea that happiness comes from living a virtuous life provides a more sustainable and meaningful approach to achieving well-being.

Boethius' thoughts on free will and determinism also resonate with modern philosophical debates. As we continue to explore the nature of human freedom and the impact of external factors on our choices, Boethius' work provides a historical perspective that enriches these discussions. His attempts to reconcile free will with divine foreknowledge offer a framework for thinking about these complex issues.

The integration of faith and reason in Boethius' work is another area of continued relevance. In a world where science and religion are often seen as opposing forces, Boethius' efforts to harmonize these ways of knowing can inspire more holistic approaches to understanding the world. His belief that reason and faith can complement each other encourages a more integrated view of knowledge.

Boethius' focus on resilience and coping with adversity is particularly pertinent in today's context. His insights into how to find strength and meaning in difficult times offer practical guidance for dealing with life's challenges. In a world facing various crises and uncertainties, Boethius' philosophy provides a source of comfort and direction.

Boethius' relevance to modern thought is evident in the enduring appeal of his ideas. His insights into happiness, virtue, free will, and the integration of different ways of knowing continue to inspire and inform contemporary discussions. Boethius' work offers valuable perspectives that can help us navigate the complexities of modern life.

## IMPACT ON WESTERN INTELLECTUAL TRADITION

Boethius' impact on the Western intellectual tradition is profound. His work served as a bridge between the ancient and medieval worlds, preserving and transmitting classical knowledge to later generations. This preservation of classical philosophy was crucial for the development of medieval thought and the eventual flowering of the Renaissance.

One of Boethius' most significant contributions was his translation and interpretation of Aristotle and Plato. These translations made the works of these ancient philosophers accessible to the Latin-speaking world. Boethius' efforts ensured that the wisdom of the ancient Greeks was not lost and could continue to influence Western thought.

Boethius' integration of classical philosophy with Christian theology also had a lasting impact. His synthesis of these traditions provided a foundation for medieval scholasticism, which sought to harmonize reason and faith. Thinkers like Thomas Aquinas built on Boethius' work, developing complex philosophical systems that have shaped Western intellectual history.

His contributions to logic and music theory were also influential. Boethius' logical works became standard texts in medieval education, laying the groundwork for later developments in logic and philosophy. His treatises on music theory helped establish the foundations of Western musical thought, influencing composers and theorists for centuries.

Boethius' work on the nature of happiness and virtue has also had a lasting impact. His ideas about the importance of inner virtues and the pursuit of the good life have continued to resonate through the ages. These concepts have influenced ethical theories and philosophical discussions on well-being and human flourishing.

Overall, Boethius' impact on the Western intellectual tradition is extensive. His efforts to preserve classical knowledge, his integration of different philosophical traditions, and his contributions to various fields have left a rich legacy. Boethius' work continues to be a vital part of the Western intellectual heritage, influencing thinkers and scholars to this day.

## PERSONAL REFLECTIONS ON BOETHIUS

Reflecting on Boethius' work, one can't help but be struck by its depth and relevance. His ability to blend personal experience with profound philosophical inquiry makes his writing both relatable and insightful. Reading "The Consolation of Philosophy" feels like having a conversation with a wise friend who understands life's challenges and offers meaningful advice.

Boethius' emphasis on inner virtues resonates deeply. In a world where external achievements often overshadow personal growth, his reminder that true happiness comes from within is powerful. This idea encourages a focus on developing character and finding fulfillment in being a good person rather than constantly chasing external success.

His reflections on fate and fortune are also thought-provoking. Boethius teaches that while we cannot control everything that happens to us, we can control how we respond. This perspective is empowering, offering a way to navigate life's unpredictability with grace and resilience. It's a reminder that our inner strength and attitude are our greatest assets.

The integration of faith and reason in Boethius' work is another aspect that stands out. He shows that these two ways of understanding the world are not mutually exclusive but can complement each other. This approach encourages a more holistic view of knowledge, where philosophical inquiry and spiritual belief can coexist and enrich one another.

Boethius' personal story adds a layer of poignancy to his philosophical insights. Knowing that he wrote "The Consolation of Philosophy" while imprisoned and facing execution gives his reflections on suffering and resilience a profound authenticity. His ability to find wisdom and peace in such dire circumstances is both inspiring and humbling.

Reflecting on Boethius' work, it's clear that his ideas offer timeless wisdom. They provide valuable guidance for navigating life's challenges, finding true happiness, and integrating different ways of knowing. Boethius' work remains a source of inspiration and insight, offering lessons that are as relevant today as they were in his own time.

## FUTURE RESEARCH DIRECTIONS

There are many promising directions for future research on Boethius. One area worth exploring further is the relationship between Boethius' personal experiences and his philosophical ideas. Investigating how his imprisonment and personal struggles influenced his work could provide deeper insights into his philosophy.

Another fruitful area of research is the impact of Boethius' translations of Aristotle and Plato on medieval thought. Scholars could examine how these translations were received and interpreted by medieval philosophers. This research could shed light on the ways in which Boethius helped shape the intellectual landscape of the Middle Ages.

The intersection of Boethius' work with other philosophical and theological traditions is also a rich field of study. Researchers could explore how Boethius' ideas were integrated into Islamic and Jewish philosophical traditions. This comparative approach could highlight the broader influence of Boethius' work across different cultures and religions.

Modern applications of Boethius' philosophy in areas like ethics, psychology, and education also warrant further investigation. Scholars could examine how his ideas about happiness, virtue, and resilience can inform contemporary practices in these fields. This research could demonstrate the practical relevance of Boethius' work in addressing modern challenges.

Additionally, new translations and interpretations of Boethius' texts could provide fresh perspectives on his work. Researchers could focus on translating lesser-known works or reinterpreting existing translations to capture nuances that may have been overlooked. This approach could make Boethius' ideas more accessible and relevant to a wider audience.

Future research on Boethius holds great promise for deepening our understanding of his contributions and exploring their relevance in contemporary contexts. By continuing to study his work, scholars can uncover new insights and keep Boethius' legacy alive and vibrant in the intellectual world.

## FINAL THOUGHTS AND REFLECTIONS

Boethius' work has stood the test of time, offering profound insights and practical guidance across the centuries. His ability to blend personal experience with philosophical inquiry creates a unique and powerful body of work that continues to resonate with readers today. Reflecting on his contributions, it's clear that Boethius' ideas remain deeply relevant and impactful.

One of the most compelling aspects of Boethius' philosophy is its focus on inner virtues and resilience. In a world full of uncertainty and change, his teachings on finding strength within and maintaining perspective are invaluable. Boethius reminds us that true happiness and fulfillment come from developing our character and staying true to our values.

His exploration of enduring philosophical questions, such as the nature of happiness, the problem of evil, and the relationship between free will and destiny, offers timeless wisdom. These questions are as relevant today as they were in Boethius' time, and his reflections provide a rich source of guidance for navigating life's complexities.

Boethius' impact on the Western intellectual tradition is undeniable. His efforts to preserve classical knowledge, integrate different philosophical traditions, and contribute to various fields have left a lasting legacy. His work continues to inspire scholars and thinkers, demonstrating the enduring power of philosophical inquiry.

As we look to the future, Boethius' ideas offer valuable insights for addressing modern challenges. His emphasis on personal growth, ethical living, and the integration of different ways of knowing provides a framework for navigating the complexities of contemporary life. Boethius' wisdom remains a vital resource for anyone seeking to lead a meaningful and fulfilling life.

In conclusion, Boethius' work is a testament to the enduring relevance and power of philosophy. His reflections on happiness, virtue, resilience, and the nature of existence offer timeless guidance. By engaging with Boethius' ideas, we can find deeper understanding and inspiration for our own lives. Boethius' legacy continues to shine brightly, offering lessons that are as relevant today as they were in his own time.

# GLOSSARY

**Adversity** - Difficult or unfavorable situations

**Allegory** - A story with a hidden meaning

**Aristotle** - Ancient Greek philosopher

**Consolation** - Comfort received after loss

**Contemplation** - Deep reflective thought

**Dialectical** - Relating to logical discussion

**Divine** - Related to a god or deity

**Evil** - Profoundly immoral and wicked

**Existential** - Relating to existence

**Faith** - Strong belief in something without proof

**Fate** - A predetermined course of events

**Fortune** - Chance or luck affecting one's life

**Free Will** - Ability to choose freely

**Happiness** - State of well-being and contentment

**Harmony** - Agreement or concord

**Justice** - Fairness in protection of rights

**Knowledge** - Facts, information, and skills acquired

**Logic** - Reasoning conducted according to principles

**Meditation** - Practice of focused thought

**Metaphysics** - Study of the nature of reality

**Moral** - Concerned with principles of right and wrong

**Music Theory** - Study of the practices of music

**Omnipotent** - All-powerful

**Philosophy** - Study of fundamental nature of knowledge

**Plato** - Ancient Greek philosopher

**Providence** - Protective care of God or nature

**Reason** - Power of the mind to think logically

**Reflection** - Serious thought or consideration

**Resilience** - Ability to recover from difficulties

**Rhetoric** - Art of effective or persuasive speaking

**Socrates** - Ancient Greek philosopher

**Solace** - Comfort in a time of distress

**Stoic** - Enduring pain without showing feelings

**Suffering** - State of undergoing pain

**Theology** - Study of the nature of God

**Tranquility** - State of being calm and peaceful

**Translation** - Process of turning text from one language to another

**Universal** - Applicable to all cases

**Value** - Importance or worth of something

**Virtue** - Behavior showing high moral standards

**Wisdom** - Quality of having knowledge and good judgment

**Wittgenstein** - 20th-century philosopher

**Wonder** - Feeling of amazement

**Worldview** - Particular philosophy of life

**Writing** - Activity of composing text

**Zenith** - The highest point reached

**Zeus** - King of the gods in Greek mythology

**Zoroastrianism** - Ancient pre-Islamic religion of Persia

**Zeitgeist** - Spirit or mood of a particular period

**Zephyr** - Gentle, mild breeze

# SUGGESTED READINGS

**Aquinas, Thomas** - *Summa Theologica*

**Aristotle** - *Nicomachean Ethics*

**Augustine, Saint** - *Confessions*

**Camus, Albert** - *The Myth of Sisyphus*

**Cicero, Marcus Tullius** - *On Duties*

**Dante Alighieri** - *The Divine Comedy*

**Descartes, René** - *Meditations on First Philosophy*

**Epicurus** - *Letters and Principal Doctrines*

**Hume, David** - *An Enquiry Concerning Human Understanding*

**Kant, Immanuel** - *Critique of Pure Reason*

**Kierkegaard, Søren** - *Fear and Trembling*

**Lewis, C.S.** - *The Problem of Pain*

**MacIntyre, Alasdair** - *After Virtue*

**Marcus Aurelius** - *Meditations*

**Nietzsche, Friedrich** - *Thus Spoke Zarathustra*

**Plato** - *The Republic*

**Rousseau, Jean-Jacques** - *The Social Contract*

**Seneca, Lucius Annaeus** - *Letters from a Stoic*

**Smith, Huston** - *The World's Religions*

**Spinoza, Baruch** - *Ethics*

Printed in Dunstable, United Kingdom

68630069R00090